FOOT in the DOOR

by John J. Pelizza, Ph.D.

Varsity Publishing
Columbus, Ohio

ACKNOWLEDGEMENT:

A special word of thanks goes to Gooley Miller, who designed the cover and spent many hours creating illustrations to make the words in this book more meaningful. His many helpful suggestions in the organization of this book will always be appreciated.

Copyright © 1985 John J. Pelizza

All rights reserved. No part of this work may be reproduced or utilized in any form or by any means, electronic or mechanical, including photocopying, microfilm and recording, or by any information storage and retrieval system without permission in writing from the publisher.

Printed in the United States of America
ISBN   0-9614872-0-8

Cover design and illustrations by Gooley Miller

Published by Varsity Publishing, a subsidiary of Varsity Sporting Goods, Columbus, Ohio.

1989 6th Edition

Produced by Coneco Laser Graphics, Inc.
Glens Falls, New York

This book is dedicated to my wife, Bonnie, whose love, support, encouragement, suggestions and patience made this book a reality. She told me I could do it — and I did.

FOOT IN THE DOOR

Foot in the Door is a practical guide to success and happiness, based on the latest research in the field of human performance. There are three key words that set the foundation for improved human performance:

Self, which is what each of us can choose to do; **Power,** the energy and drive that is within us waiting to be tapped; and **Concepts,** ideas that will guide us in our search for success and happiness. Put them all together and you have **Self-Power Concepts**, a new way of reacting to your environment.

You will be amazed at your personal and professional growth as you begin applying **Self-Power Concepts** to your daily living. When you apply these concepts they will put you into a positive growth pattern that is exciting, growth producing, and never-ending. With this in mind let us begin.

Table of Contents

How to Read This Book		ix
SELF-POWER CONCEPTS: An Overview		xi
CHAPTER I	Introduction to Self-Power	1
CHAPTER II	Self-Assessment	14
CHAPTER III	Becoming a Positive Thinker	21
CHAPTER IV	Identifying and Setting Life Goals	34
CHAPTER V	Goal Setting	50
CHAPTER VI	Failure Will Lead to Success if You Allow It	64
CHAPTER VII	Dealing with Stress as a Positive and Productive Force in Your Life	69
CHAPTER VIII	How to Use Your Creative Imagination for Your Personal and Professional Growth	84
CHAPTER IX	A Self-Confidence Formula for You	108
CHAPTER X	High Performance Characteristics of Self-Powered Individuals	113
CHAPTER XI	Time Management	122
CHAPTER XII	Ten Principles of Self-Power Living	136

HOW TO READ THIS BOOK

Self-Power Concepts is about you. Becoming a **Self-Power Person** takes time and hard work. As you read this book, select the principles you are willing to put into action. Your personal and professional growth depends upon how much you are willing to apply. The more you apply, the greater your growth.

You will learn, as you read this book, that the key to personal and professional growth is action. The more action, the more growth. There is no growth in inertia. Hence, I strongly urge you to **become actively involved** while you read this book. Make notes in the margins, in the middle of the page, on the top and the bottom, in all of the blank spaces and between the lines. Carry out each of the **Self-Power Activities** which are designed to help you grow personally and professionally. Make this book your own personal notebook. Add to it. Cross things out. Talk to the book. Let it respond to you. Make it your friend. Allow it to become a map for your personal and professional growth.

I can assure you the journey you are about to take will be one of excitement, thrills, and great growth.

Enjoy!

SELF-POWER CONCEPTS: AN OVERVIEW

Conceptually, **Self-Power Concepts** is an innovative approach to assist you in leading a positive and productive life. To state it another way, **Self-Power Concepts** is designed to help you become and stay happy.

A basic premise of **Self-Power** recognizes that one must assume increasing responsibilities for one's own well-being. The foundation of the program is based on building a positive self-image. Content is arranged in such a way as to permit you to become increasingly aware of the control you can exercise over your own well-being, which will lead to a heightened awareness of your "self-power".

The purpose of this book is to teach you the concepts and applications of **Self-Power** so you can learn to grow personally and professionally to become a happier person.

As you read this book, you will be asked to participate in a variety of application activities that will get you involved personally. These activities are designed specifically to assist you in becoming a **Self-Powered Person**. You will discover many things about yourself. These discoveries will help you in identifying your life goals and, most important, in achieving them.

The ultimate objective of this book is to provide you with the appropriate knowledge and skills so you can become a **Self-Powered Person** in order to achieve and maintain a high level of happiness in your life.

Assuming you are willing to apply the concepts and ideas that are to follow, I can assure you that at the completion of this book you will have learned how to utilize **Self-Power Concepts** as a powerful and productive force in your life. You will become a positive thinker, be able to deal with stress in a productive and positive way, set goals and accomplish them, deal with failure so that it becomes a positive force rather than a negative one, develop leadership skills that allow you to help yourself so you can share and help others, utilize an affirmation process that will attract you to your goals in an easy fashion, grow in confidence so you will be willing to take steps and strides forward that you were unwilling to take before and, finally, develop effective time management skills so you can use every moment of your life in a positive and productive manner.

At this point I would like to ask you a question: Do you need **Self-Power Concepts**? Take the following **Self-Power Concepts** survey. See what you find out. *Write your answers in the space provided.*

QUESTION 1: Are you really happy and satisfied with your personal and professional life?_____

QUESTION 2: Do you get excited when you think about daily activities and where these activities are leading you?_____

QUESTION 3: Are you satisfied with your self-confidence level?_____

QUESTION 4: Are you utilizing the stress in your life in a positive and productive manner?_____

QUESTION 5: Are you setting and achieving personal and professional goals?_____

QUESTION 6: Are you happy with who you are and where you are going?_____

QUESTION 7: Do you know what you stand for?_____

If your answer to any of these questions was "no," I believe this book can be of tremendous value to you.

I would like to suggest that you implement the following **Self-Power** action plans to help you to begin moving in a positive direction:

1. Go for a walk. Think about the things you wanted to become in your childhood. What happened to your childhood belief and enthusiasm?
2. Set aside 15 to 20 minutes each day to relax and imagine yourself achieving and enjoying the attainment of your goals.
3. Find something positive in each of your personal and professional relationships.
4. DO IT NOW!

What are the specific objectives of this book?

1. This book is for you and about you.
2. This book is to help you grow personally and professionally.
3. This book is to help you identify what you want in life so

you can feel it. This will help you to attain it.

4. This book is designed to get you moving if you are stuck!

What are the assumptions of **Self-Power Concepts**? Each of us can grow personally and professionally at any age in the life cycle.

Each of us has the **Self-Power** to be in control of our lives.

Each of us has the **Self-Power** to change positively if we choose.

Each of us has a lot of potential we are not presently using.

Each of us can become the person we really want to be.

Self-Power Concepts has worked for me and my family and for the many participants who have gone through my **Self-Power Concepts** seminars. I am sure **Self-Power Concepts** can make a difference in your life.

Read the material; apply the ideas; become the person you really want to be.

Chapter I

Introduction to Self-Power

Are you ready for a major change in your life? Then put a little **SPC** in it! Don't look for it at your local drugstore. It's not for sale. It's a new kind of program. It is the way to a new YOU . . . a way to unleash your latent **Self-Power**.

For skeptics, **SPC** or **Self-Power Concepts** is something of a surprise, for there are no Madison Avenue claims, no money-back guarantees. All of your life's problems don't suddenly disappear through the **Self-Power** process. For the optimist looking for an easy answer, it's disappointing to discover that **SPC** is effective only for persons who truly want to invest time, effort and energy in order to grow. **Self-Power Concepts** is a proven program that works for individuals who work and implement the program.

Foot in the Door

For ordinary people who realize that they are not living up to their full potential, **SPC** is a great program. It is exactly the right program for you if you have been meaning to do something about a gnawing, knotty problem or a whole bag of tired old ones you have been coping with unsuccessfully in your personal and professional life.

Even if you are lucky enough to be between crises at the moment and there are no critical personal or professional issues tearing your tranquility apart, **SPC** is special. Essentially, **Self-Power** is a new formula, a concept, a different theme, a claim about a latent power. Let's examine the concept more critically and coldly calculate its merit, for we live in a world of charlatans and hucksters and must always be sure of the service we buy.

Self-Power Defined

By definition **Self-Power Concepts** refers to a body of knowledge or concepts about one's capacity to grow. The origin of **Self-Power** is somewhat obscure — probably it always existed like an idea without form, a concept that hasn't yet crystallized. Perhaps it existed as a notion, a recurring truism that self is the key ingredient in the resolution of one's problems. More nearly, **Self-Power** as a system evolved over time until it became possible to identify and analyze its basic components, to study the process objectively, and to begin to apply **Self-Power Concepts** to life situations.

Theoretically, **Self-Power** refers to a body of knowledge or concepts about one's capacity to grow personally and professionally. **Self-Power** focuses on and fuses two separate concepts. The first states that the key ingredient in the resolution of an issue is the person trying to grow. The other dimension contained in the theory is the notion that within each of us is a latent power which, if harnessed and channeled correctly, would in effect contribute to a new you or me or us as **Self-Powered** individuals.

Before committing oneself to learning the **Self-Power** theory, ask yourself these two questions:

Do I want to think positively and effectively?_____

Do I want to set goals that work?_____

Ask still another question: Do I want to grow?_____

The rewards are great for those who do. The benefits can be summarized in the formula K plus A equals BB.

K plus A equals BB is not a geometric equation. It's a **Self-Power** rule that, when translated, reads: If you start with *knowledge*, understanding and facts, add your personal effort, *action* and application, the chemical reaction will result in *big benefits* to you both personally and professionally.

Basic Assumptions

For **Self-Power** to work, one must accept four basic assumptions:

The first assumption is that every person can grow personally.

The second assumption is that every person can grow personally because of an internal power each of us possesses. Everyone has the self-power to change. At the gut level, right now, are you not aware that you are not operating at 100 percent efficiency, not realizing your full potential?

The third assumption flows from the first two. If you believe that you have the ability to grow personally and have the capacity to change, then it follows that each of us has the power to be in control of our lives.

Finally, the fourth assumption to become a self-powered person states that we have little or no control over events in our lives, but total control over the way we react to events.

Restating these four basic assumptions, **Self-Power** asserts that each of us has the ability to grow, the self-power to change, the capacity to be in control of our lives, and the total control over the way we react to the unforeseen events in our lives.

Let me illustrate these four principles with a true story. Bill was a teen-ager in high school and was required to take a series of examinations given by school counselors. At the completion of these tests the counselors advised his parents that they would be wasting their money if they sent him to college. At this juncture in Bill's life he was told by so-called "educated counselors" that he had poor academic ability. Most likely the tests that were analyzed indicated shortcomings in several academic areas. However, the serious error made by the counselors was telling Bill and his parents that he should not be allowed to go to college and that he had little ability or potential in pursuing an academic career. At this stage in Bill's life he applied Assumption No. 1 which is: *everyone can grow personally and professionally.* When Bill learned that the counselors' recommendation was that he not go to college because of low academic test scores, he began to utilize his inner resources to develop skills in academics. As a result he was accepted to a college and continued on in college until he received several graduate degrees. **Fantastic.**

The second assumption states that *everyone has the Self-Power to change.* Here, again, this can be illustrated by Bill's willingness to change his thinking about academics and to acquire additional skills so that he could pursue a degree in college.

The third assumption can be illustrated in this example by the fact that Bill had the control to decide whether or not he would believe the counselors. Fortunately he chose to believe in himself and went ahead and pursued a successful college career. Believing in yourself can make all the difference in your life. So *don't be afraid to believe in yourself.*

Foot in the Door

The final assumption in the **Self-Power** formula states that *we have the total control over the way we react to events in our lives.* Here again, at this particular point in Bill's life he chose to react positively to a potentially negative situation. As a result, Bill achieved the following academic degrees:

> Associate Arts and Science Degree
> Bachelor of Science Degree
> Masters Degree
> Doctor of Philosophy Degree

Can you think of a similar story in your own life that demonstrates these four principles? As you review the events associated with your story ask yourself: How did I grow from this experience? Or, how could I have grown from this situation? The key is how you choose to THINK.

YOU'LL GROW BEYOND YOUR PRESENT PERCEPTION

The major point I would like to crystallize at this time is that all of us have the ability to grow far beyond our present perception of ourselves. It is a critical point to understand. It is important that each individual realizes that none of us knows our potential, but that each of us can set action plans in motion which will allow us to evolve and develop to far greater heights than we can visualize now. This is a fact, not just a theory. Ask yourself this question: How many skills, abilities and insights do I have today that at one point I did not have? If you analyze how you achieved your skills, you basically went through a systematic approach (which will be discussed later) that allowed you to grow personally and professionally. Hence, it is clear to me that individuals need to choose to be **Self-Powered**. They need to choose to become what they are capable of becoming. By doing this, an individual becomes a dynamic force capable of taking actions to achieve his or her goals. In the process of taking action the individual will become happier and feel fulfillment. In essence, this is what a **Self-Powered Person** does. They light up their own lives so that in effect they can light up the lives of those around them.

At this point I would like you to participate in the following activity:

1. Why are you reading this book?_____
   _____

2. What are your expectations as a result of reading this book for personal and professional growth?_____
   _____

3. List two major successes you have had in your life already and then pat yourself on the back._____

Foot in the Door

4. Identify two major stresses that are occuring in your life right now. _____

5. Write down any ideas you have gained from reading Chapter I that you can apply to help yourself grow personally and professionally. _____

_____
_____
_____
_____
_____
_____
_____
_____

As you review your responses to questions 1 through 4, see what you have learned about yourself. Make some notes.

_____
_____
_____

Introduction to Self-Power

As you proceed in this book, I will teach you how to grow personally and professionally. I will show you how to utilize past successes and failures to attain future successes. I will illustrate and demonstrate how you can take stress and utilize it as a productive force in your life and, finally, you will see as you read each chapter in this book how you can apply the ideas so you can become the person you really want to be.

The following **Self-Power** activity is especially for you. The title of this activity is "Excelling, Achieving, Growing." Start now to implement the positive action plan that follows:

> I am going to suggest that you keep a daily diary. In your daily personal diary note the degree to which you are able to implement an action plan or to change a particular behavior. That's right, I would suggest you keep a personal diary for the next month or two. Apply the concepts and ideas. See the actions that occur and the benefits that result to you personally.

Foot in the Door

The diary will be a constant reinforcement of your personal and professional growth. It will turn you on. It will juice you up. It will give you meaning and purpose to your life. I strongly urge you to keep the diary. However, that's your decision. Again, it's your decision as to whether or not you want to grow personally and professionally. When I have worked with clients, I have found that keeping the diary is critical to personal and professional growth.

Don't be overwhelmed trying to do all of the things that I am going to suggest in this activity. If it's easier, start with one goal, focus on that main objective until you achieve it. Resist the temptation to postpone getting started. Here, then, is your positive **Self-Power** action plan:

1. Wake up happy. Tell yourself it will be a great day! Optimism and pessimism are learned behavioral attitudes. One of the best ways to develop a positive attitude is to start early in life or at least early on any given day to practice the desired behavior. For example, wake up to music; sing in the shower; be glad you're alive. Identify

a specific action plan that is your way of getting the day off to a good start.

2. Find something positive in all of your personal relationships. Accentuate the positive benefits in even the most trying circumstances. Record an example in your diary today of your having made the effort to see the positive.

3. Look at problems as opportunities. Make a list of your most pressing problems — the ones that interfere with your personal or professional growth. Write a one-sentence description of the problem. Now, rewrite the description, reviewing it as an opportunity to exercise your creativity and ingenuity as a counselor. View the solution as if you were advising one of your best friends.

Example:
Problem: I am gaining too much weight.
Opportunity: I will learn to eat properly and exercise in order to lose weight.

_____
_____
_____
_____
_____
_____
_____
_____
_____
_____
_____

Foot in the Door

_____

_____

_____

4. Be happy with your health status. Cure what's curable. Prevent what's preventable and enjoy the rest. Is it time for a periodic physical checkup to get you headed in the right direction? If the answer if yes, have the checkup.

5. Expect the best from yourself and others. Two of the keys to effective leadership are encouragement and praise. Verbalize on a daily basis your optimistic attitude toward yourself, your family and your friends.

Well that's your first **Self-Power** action plan. The more actions you take relative to the action plan suggested, the quicker your personal and professional growth will take place. How do I know? Because I've used them. Past participants have used them, and I can tell you, they work! I am not going to wish you luck because luck has nothing to do with it. It is a matter of following the action plans over which you have total control that will result in your growing personally and professionally and, most important, which will result in making you a happier individual.

Write down Key Ideas you have learned in this section. For each idea write a positive action you can take to put yourself into a positive growth pattern.

_____

_____

Introduction to Self-Power

Chapter II

Self-Assessment

I would like to begin this chapter with a **Self-Power** activity that is designed to provide you, the reader, with a personal profile of yourself. Answer the following six questions thoughtfully. The answers will help you see yourself as you are at the beginning of this book. Reviewing your answers during and after you read this book will help you determine the degree to which your behavior has changed and the extent to which you have become a **Self-Powered Person.** In answering each question, list one example that will help support or illustrate your answer. Avoid self-criticism.

Self-Power Concepts Assessment Activity:

1. Are you usually optimistic about all aspects of your life?
   _____

Example:_____

2. Do you expect a high level of wellness for yourself?____
   Example:_____

3. Are you easily discouraged and down on yourself?____
   Example:_____

4. Do you view personal problems as potential opportunities for personal growth?_____
   Example:_____

5. Do you tend to criticize others rather than to praise?____
   Example:_____

6. Do some of the answers to the questions above suggest an image or behavior you would like to improve?_____
   Example:_____

When you have finished answering these six questions, ask yourself: What have I learned? Write it down now.

_____
_____
_____
_____

Foot in the Door

_____

_____

_____

_____

How can I use what I have learned to help myself grow? Write it down now.

_____

_____

_____

_____

_____

_____

_____

_____

Am I correct that your answer to Question Six is "yes"? *Good!* Lets move on.

While you read this book and apply concepts within it, you will learn how to modify your behavior through the power of positive thinking, effective goal setting, efficient time management, use of affirmations and other **Self-Power** skills.

Self-Assessment

While I can describe the process for becoming a **Self-Powered Person** it is really up to you to decide what concepts, if any, are applicable to your personal and professional growth. You also must ask yourself how much time and effort you are willing to put into your life. I believe the mere fact that you are sitting down and reading this book indicates that you are willing to put time and effort into your personal and professional growth. Believe me, when you apply these principles, you will see a major change take place in your life.

One of the best ways to measure personal growth is to continue your diary during the time you are reading this book and applying its principles. This diary will record your activities and show your progress toward becoming a **Self-Powered Person**. Since not all ideas are right or work for everyone, note those **Self-Power Concepts** that work best for you and use them frequently and consistently. Please note that the diary is for your own personal use. As a chronicle it should reveal the degree to which

Foot in the Door

you have attempted to incorporate **Self-Power Concepts** into your personal and professional life.

If you answered "no" to any of the questions in the ASSESSMENT ACTIVITY, you may seriously want to consider implementing the following **Self-Power** Actions:

Self-Power Positive Action Plans:
1. Take the blame and the credit for where you are in life.
2. Instead of saying "*I have to,*" use the concept "*I've decided to.*"
3. Use the following motto in your daily transactions: *My rewards in life will reflect my service and contribution.*
4. Another idea to keep you growing personally and professionally — TNT. Today, not tomorrow.
5. Look in the mirror and see if you are the person you really want to be.

These positive action plans work when you work the plans. Remember, the sooner you decide to get into action, the sooner you will receive big benefits.

Self-Assessment

Write down Key Ideas you have learned about yourself from this chapter. For each idea write down a positive action you can take to put yourself into a positive growth pattern.

Foot in the Door

Chapter III

Becoming a Positive Thinker

Let's stop a minute to restate the purpose of our mission. Simply stated, our goal is to help a person become self-powered. **Self-Power Concepts** offers the individual the opportunity to have complete control and teaches the techniques and skills necessary to accomplish that goal. **Self-Power** also says very candidly that it's all up to you. You decide. It's your life, your investment, your reward.

Try the following activity entitled "It's All Up to You." This activity provides a timeout to get in touch with yourself. Answer these five questions candidly:

1. What do you fear most in life?_____

_____
_____

2. How does that fear impact on your personal or professional life? _____
   _____
   _____

3. What do you want most from life at the present time? __
   _____
   _____

4. Do you concentrate all or most of your energy and attention on attaining the goals you desire most? _____
   _____
   _____

5. Do you think more about the rewards of success or the penalties for failure? _____
   _____
   _____

Summarize what you have learned.

_____
_____
_____
_____
_____
_____
_____

_____

_____

_____

_____

_____

These questions should give you something to think about. After completing the activity, it's all up to you. Think about the following statements other participants have made as a result of going through the **Self-Power Concepts** Program:

Participant Responses:

A positive mental attitude is a key modality in attaining one's goals.

Act decisively.

Take an Action.

Give praise.

Go for it.

I control my thinking.

I love being in a positive growth pattern.

It now is essential that we move on to the task of acquiring those skills that will allow us to become **Self-Powered**.

A Formula for Positive Thinking:

There are three essential skills inherent in the concept of positive thinking that are an intergal part of becoming a **Self-Powered Person.** They are:

1. You must think of something positive to say to everyone you interact with, not just the people you admire, love or respect, but really think of something positive to say about everyone. That means the neighbor you haven't spoken to in five years, the boss you despise, the teacher you can't stand. Think of something positive. Come on, now. You can! Every person has at least one redeeming quality.

2. You must learn to see something positive in everything that happens to you. Yes, I know, you want to reject that principle. You can think of special circumstances and disasters, for example, in which no one could reasonably be expected to see the positive. But look at it this way. You have a choice. You can interpret a situation negatively or you can look for the one aspect, the single

dimension, the significant factor in that same scenario which provides the basis for optimism and for hope. If you are serious about becoming a **Self-Powered Person**, you have to learn ownership. Remember the basic assumption that said we have little or no control over events in our lives, but total control over the way we react to events? Do you see the inter-relatedness of these two pieces of the puzzle? In combination they can be restated as follows:

> Of the events in our lives over which we have no control, **Self-Powered Persons** find something positive in everything that happens.

Essentially, then, **Self-Power** demands not only that one say something positive, but also perceives all events as having a positive value. The challenge is this: *Do you want to change? Are you willing to take the action? Do you believe in self-responsibility? Do you really want to act self-confidently? Do you own it? Do you know who you are and where you are going?*

Quite probably, there are some individuals who are content with their present environment, suspended in what is called "the comfort zone," where there may be security but little or no growth. Restating the **Self-Power** position, the philosophy is simple; its doctrine is positive. It encourages you to see the positive element in both persons and events. You can find those elements if you look purposely, actively, intentionally and intelligently. You make the choice. You have the power. You have total control over how you react.

3. There still is one more dimension to consider. In addition to saying the positive and seeing the positive, one must

also learn the third skill, which is to develop and activate simple plans to achieve one's goals. These, then, are the three key points: (1) say something positive to everyone with whom you interact; (2) see something positive in every event; (3) develop and activate simple plans to achieve them.

It has been reported very accurately that the biggest handicap one can encounter is not in the evil forces that abound in the world, but in the negative forces between your own ears. Many people think or believe that they cannot, and so they do not. **Self-Power** promises you can if you want to.

Many times when doing **Self-Power** seminars, participants have a difficult time accepting the positive thinking formula. Hence, there always are those participants who will do their best, utilize a great deal of energy, to disprove the concept. Typically, a participant will throw this question out to see whether or not the principles of positive thinking in fact work: "How do you go about being a positive thinker when there has been a death in the family?" Let's provide the following illustration to show the application of positive thinking.

Let's assume a seventeen-year-old boy in perfect health is standing on a corner and a car goes out of control and kills him. What parts of the positive thinking model can be utilized in this situation? I believe Part 2 is most applicable in this situation. You must learn to see something positive in everything that happens to you. Let me explain. Is it not true that the immediate family and friends would go through the process of grief and loss? Is it not true that these same individuals would learn what grief and loss is all about and would therefore be in a better position to empathize with others in the future who suffer serious loss? Is it not true that these individuals might respect, cherish and value their current personal relationships more as a result of such a tragedy? Is it not true that these individuals probably would learn to value and cherish life more?

As you can see, there are many positives which can result from such a tragedy, but only if one looks for them and accepts them. This is not to say that their grief and loss are eliminated for, in fact, they will continue to exist. However, by identifying the positive aspects of the situation the individual is in a better position to get through difficult situations. Thus, being a positive thinker, even in this extreme example, is possible. Not only is it possible, it is advisable if an individual wants to maintain good mental and physical health. Remember, those who are close to the deceased need to get on with living. They need to get on with helping those who also were close to the deceased and they cannot do this if they have serious mental and physical problems

Foot in the Door

because they are dwelling on the negative loss. Here again, the power of positive thinking can be the guiding light in helping the survivors get through this traumatic situation. Folks, positive thinking works! It works in small situations, in grave situations; it just flat out works! The key, then, is to learn the principles, apply the principles, and see what happens. You will be pleasantly surprised.

The following is a **Self-Power** activity entitled "Seeing the Positive."

Write down five things that occurred to you during the past week that were positive.

_____
_____
_____
_____
_____
_____
_____
_____
_____
_____
_____
_____
_____
_____

Now you might say nothing positive has happened. Well, let's take a look at this situation. Did you have a good dinner or breakfast during the past week? Did you get a smile from someone? Did someone praise you for something you did well? Did you smell any flowers or see a sunset? Did you listen to good music? Did you have some time for yourself to meditate and think? As you can see, one could go on and on with all of the positive things that are occurring around us. However, they are not positive unless we see them, feel them, touch them, recognize them, integrate them into our being. A positive thinker seeks them out. It gives positive thinkers the energy and drive to go forward in the things they want to become. Can you think of some others now? I'll bet you can!

Next is an activity we call "For the Skeptics." One of the basic tenets of becoming a positive thinker is to learn to **see something positive** in everything that happens to you. To apply this concept to real life, complete the following activity:

Foot in the Door

Select and review a personal crisis you experienced that had many negative qualities. Identify at least two positive aspects of this experience. Remember, to complete this activity you must keep looking until you find two positive aspects to this experience. This activity is similar to the illustration I gave you about the young boy who was killed by an automobile.

Personal Crisis

Describe: _____
_____
_____
_____

Positive Aspects:

1. _____
_____
_____
_____
_____

2. _____
_____
_____
_____
_____

Here is a **Self-Power** Positive Action Plan:

Starting today and for the next 7 consecutive days, keep a log in which you record the following data (this can be done in your daily diary):

Identify something positive about a different person on each of the next 7 days. Discuss the particular quality that you have noted with each person. Record in your log how you felt during the discussion and the other person's reaction.

At the end of the week summarize your feelings about this activity.

Identify the benefits that you derived and ask yourself how you have grown personally as a result of this activity.

Let me assure you that this is a fun activity. It will prove to you that positive thinking really works and that you have total control over the process.

Some Self-Powered Generalizations:

1. In becoming a **Self-Powered Person**, you will have to be willing to deal with failure, to cope with setbacks, and to take some risks.
2. Successful individuals perceive disappointments, setbacks, and failures only as slight detours.
3. No one is perfect.

4. Learn to deal with failure by seeing the positive aspects that you have learned from the failure. When you begin to think like this, you will no longer fear failure. **Wow!**
5. Always look for the good in a situation.
6. When you identify something negative in a situation, develop an action plan to deal with it and put it into action.
7. Think positively. Don't get caught up in setting limits for someone else or yourself. Stop telling people they can't. Stop creating artificial barriers for yourself, too.

Each facet of **Self-Power Concepts** fits together like a piece of a jigsaw puzzle. For the puzzle to be complete, no piece can be missing. The next chapter is "Goal Setting," which is an integral part of the **Self-Power Program.**

Write down the New Ideas you have learned from becoming a positive thinker. For each idea write down a positive action you can take to put yourself into a positive growth pattern.

_____
_____
_____
_____
_____
_____
_____
_____

Becoming a Positive Thinker

Chapter IV

Identifying and Setting Life Goals

Before you can implement the concept of **Self-Power** for maximum benefits, it is vital that you identify and list your life goals. The reason for this is simple. Once an individual identifies life goals, he or she has direction. Once you have direction, your energies can be focused in that area so that you have the capacity to achieve your goals. Another way of saying this is that once you have direction, it will lead to persistent, hard work and over a period of time this will culminate in your achieving your goals.

At this point let me clarify what I mean by life goals. While it is true that I am talking about major goals in your life such as becoming a physician, a ballerina, owning a home on 100 acres, taking a trip around the world, owning your own sailboat, writing a book or having a happy family with three children, other lifetime goals can be smaller in nature. For example, learning to swim, to ride a bicycle, to play racquetball, to dance, earning a degree, planting a garden, losing weight, improving your fitness level and so on. What is critical is that individuals have goals that get them excited and enthusiastic. Typically, large life goals will allow any individual to get excited. Most people, however, are afraid to think of major life goals because they fear not attaining them. What this does is cause people to identify life goals that are not important to them. Hence, they put their energies into life goals that are not the ones they really want. Consequently, they are not as enthusiastic as they could be. To be perfectly candid, most people never really sit down to identify their life goals. What they do instead is learn how to survive and just "get by." Those individuals who dedicate their lives to just surviving and "getting by" typically are never happy. This makes sense because they are not moving in a direction toward something they really want. For this reason I cannot overstate the need to take time out and put energy into identifying your life goals. This will make a critical difference in how you function daily.

Let me illustrate how life goals can produce excitement and enthusiasm in your life. I remember when I was a young boy of eight years old I always wanted to go fishing on a boat. Up until that time, however, I never had the opportunity to go fishing on a boat. One day a neighbor in the apartment house I lived in asked my mother if it would be all right for him to take me out on his boat fishing. When my mother informed me of this and said that I had her permission to go with him, I could not sleep for three days. Wow! Let's analyze the process. At that point in time a life goal for me was going to take place. I was looking forward to it and I had a great deal of excitement and enthusiasm in me. It should also be noted that there was a good deal of excitement and enthusiasm in me even when I did not know that I was going on the fishing trip with my neighbor. The mere fact that I had identified a life goal and thought about it frequently got me excited. Are you getting the picture? Identify your life goals and you will perk up because you now have direction and, more importantly, you are working toward something you really want.

Point of caution: Stop listening to all of the people who tell you that you can't, shouldn't or it is not realistic. Identify and set those life goals that are important to you. Apply action and watch what happens. It is **taking the actions** that will produce success and happiness in your life.

Let me put it another way. Do you know any people who are down and depressed? I'll bet they have no life goals to look forward to and, more importantly, they have no life goals with action plans that they are implementing.

On the other hand, do you know people who tend always to be up, excited, happy and feeling good about themselves? If you do, I will bet they have some life goals they are working toward and it is this very factor, the process of action, the identification of the life goal, that is producing the juice and joy in their lives.

At this point you have to decide what you are going to do. If you choose to be a **Self-Powered Person**, you will choose to put the energy and time into identifying those life goals.

How Do You Identify And Set Life Goals?

It's easy!

1. Find a quiet place where you can relax and be by yourself. Take a walk. Lie on the couch. Sit in a chair. Watch a sunset. Get the picture?
2. Think of all the things you have wanted to do or become when you were very young and even now — that's right; trust me; this really works. Don't worry about how you will achieve your life goals. Just identify them by dreaming, visualizing and seeing visions of what you want.
3. As you identify your life goals, write them down. That's all there is to it. In the space provided, list some of your life goals as specifically as you can, both large and small. Once you have developed a list of life goals and begin to think about the possibility of attaining them, I can assure you that you will begin to get excited. It is this very excitement that will drive you and provide you with the necessary energy that will be required to achieve your life goals.

Foot in the Door

In the space provided write down your life goals.

LIFE GOALS

Identifying and Setting Life Goals

Once you have identified and listed your life goals, ask yourself the following question: **How many of my life goals fit into the following six categories?**

>Occupational
>Recreational
>Physical
>Mental
>Spiritual
>Social

I will suggest that you and I should be setting life goals in each of these categories. This will create balance in our lives and make us strong. The following picture illustrates this point.

Which House Would You Rather Live In?

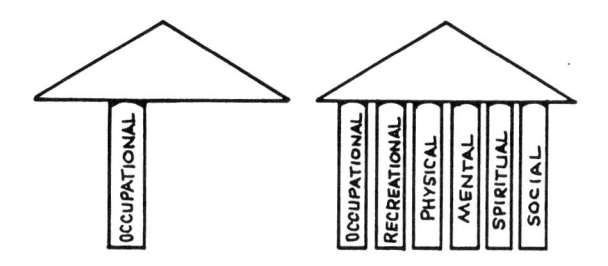

GET THE IDEA!

As I have already stated, the **Self-Powered Person** sets life goals in each of these areas. This is vital. If you concentrate only in one area, you will be out of balance and unhappy. For example, there are many individuals who are financially prosperous; however, they may not be happy. Possibly you know someone who is extremely intelligent, highly successful in his or her career, but is excessively overweight and has a cardiovascular problem which causes a great deal of distress in that person's life. As you can see, the key is balance. You need to be working in each of the six life areas so that your life has balance which will allow you to propel yourself in any direction you choose and achieve any life goal you desire. Remember, where there is balance there is strength. Where there is strength there is confidence. Where there is confidence there is a desire and the guts to go for the life goal. Finally, the process of doing these things is what makes your life meaningful and produces happiness. Get the picture?

The next step is to review your life goals. For each life goal write down the specific action plan you have for accomplishing the goal. If you don't have any plans now take some time to develop them and then write them down. Once you do this it will make you feel terrific because you now have a destination. Each destination will produce energy and drive within you which will assist you in achieving your life goals. **Wow!**

Action Plans For Life Goals

Occupational _____

_____
_____
_____
_____
_____

Recreational _____

_____
_____
_____
_____
_____

Physical _____

_____
_____
_____
_____
_____
_____

Mental_____

_____
_____
_____
_____
_____
_____

Spiritual_____

_____
_____
_____
_____
_____
_____

Social_____

_____
_____
_____
_____
_____
_____
_____

Finally, if you are doing things in some of your life areas that are not contributing to your life goals, you may want seriously to consider deleting them. You have to take some time and make some tough decisions. Think it through and then proceed.

Remember, if you are serious and willing to commit to your life goals, then you will make the appropriate adjustment in each of the six life areas so you can move toward achieving your life goals. If you want to prove this to yourself, think of something in your life that you worked very hard to achieve. Reflect back on the events leading to your success and I will guarantee you that the time, effort and sweat that you put into achieving your goal as you review it now was well worth it.

As you keep thinking about it, you probably will begin to feel good about it. Wouldn't it be fantastic to have a list of future goals that turn you on, make you feel good, get you juiced, so that, when you begin each day, you've got something to look forward to and a happy outlook on life? Well, the key is identifying your life goals and setting some action plans in motion to achieve them.

Finally, I can't stress too strongly how important it is for you to spend whatever time it takes to identify and write down your life goals. Once this is accomplished, you will feel great and be on your way to fulfilling your life goals. This can be a super exciting experience.

Now you are ready to rewrite your life goals and for each one write down your action plan.

Life Goals and Action Plans

Occupational Goals and Action Plans

_____

Recreational Goals and Action Plans

_____

Physical Goals and Action Plans_____

_____
_____
_____
_____
_____
_____
_____
_____
_____
_____

Mental Goals and Action Plans_____

_____
_____
_____
_____
_____
_____
_____
_____
_____
_____
_____

Spiritual Goals and Action Plans_____

_____
_____
_____
_____
_____
_____
_____
_____
_____
_____

Social Goals and Action Plans_____

_____
_____
_____
_____
_____
_____
_____
_____
_____
_____
_____

Ask yourself the following questions:

1. Do you know your life goals?
2. Are your life goals written down?
3. Do you have an action plan for achieving your life goals?
4. Are you implementing your action plans on a daily basis to achieve your life goals?
5. Do you repeat your life goals to yourself twice a day?

If you answered "no" to any of these questions take an action so you can turn the "no" to a "yes." This will put you in motion and make you feel better. Finally, focus your attention and energy on the accomplishments of your life goals. Forget about the consequences of failure. Remember, most people get what they think about most. You begin thinking about your life goals and fantastic things will begin to happen.

In Chapter V I will explain a goal-setting formula that works if you work the formula. Once your life goals are identified, you can utilize the goal-setting formula to achieve them; but always remember, *the key is the identification of your life goal.*

Once you have your list of life goals, you will be on your way. A good test to determine whether or not your list of life goals is real, effective and true is to read the list to yourself. If you do not get excited about the list, you've got the wrong list and you can be assured you probably will not achieve those life goals. However, if when you read your list you get excited, the chances of your achieving them are quite high. This, of course, is assuming you are willing to pay the price to achieve them.

Summary

We've come a long way together, reading, talking and thinking about **Self-Power**. I would like to share with you a special message about the program. My phone rang one day recently. It was a lady who had attended one of my **Self-Power** seminars and had applied **Self-Power Concepts** to a very stressful employment situation. The reason Joan called me was to say, "It works! I called to tell you it really works! This program has helped me so much. It's wonderful to feel this way!" **Self-Power** can help you, but only to the extent that you are willing to take an action. There is no growth in inertia. We must all recognize that we determine our actions. My recommendation is to go for it.

Write down the Key Ideas you have learned from identifying and writing down your life goals and action plans. For each idea write down a positive action you can take to put yourself into a positive growth pattern.

Identifying and Setting Life Goals

Chapter V

Goal-Setting

What is goal-setting? The process of goal-setting is one which allows an individual to move himself or herself in a preconceived direction.

Let me put it another way. The purpose of setting goals is to allow an individual to move and to grow in those directions he or she chooses. Some people will tell you that goal-setting doesn't work. I have found in my experience that those who say goal-setting doesn't work are those who either use goal-setting formulas that are incorrect or who don't work the goal-setting formula.

In this chapter I will present to you a goal-setting model that absolutely works if you work the formula. Here are the components of the goal-setting formula:

1. ***Identify your vision, dream or want.*** It is imperative for you to be able to visualize what you want, what you dream about, what your future vision is for yourself. The reason for this is simple. By identifying your dreams, wants, and visions, you will create an emotional charge that will propel you toward your goal. Let me illustrate. When working with clients in goal-setting, I normally ask them to list 2-5 things they want or 2-5 things they have always dreamed about or 2-5 things they have a vision of. After they identify these areas, I can determine whether the client has identified something that, in fact, is what he or she really wants. The way I do this is to watch the emotional impact the items have on the clients as they discuss them. If the items are real, the client will express emotion while communicating them to me. This emotion can be recognized in the clients' speech, non-verbal cues and the glitter in their eyes. Once the individual has set his or her vision, identified the dream or want, it is time to set a specific goal.

2. ***State your goal.*** In stating your goal, it should have the following characteristics:

   a) It should be specific. For example, if you say you want to lose weight, that's not specific enough. What needs to be said is that you would like to lose ten pounds.

   b) Write down the goal. It is imperative that the goal be written down so that you know exactly what you want.

   c) Put a date on your goal. The purpose for putting a date for the completion of the goal is to provide you with urgency.

   d) Repeat the goal every day. The reason for this is that

it will make an impression on your mind and thus become a predominant thought which will guide you toward the goal.

e) Share your goal with someone close to you who will support you in your endeavor.

By stating your goal as I have indicated above, you have a clear and precise direction as to where you are going. The only thing that needs to be done now is to follow the plan you have developed.

3. *List all the benefits.* In this section you need to list all of the benefits you will derive once you have completed your goal. It is imperative that you take time to list these benefits on paper because you will use this information later.

4. *Describe your action plan.* Write down specifically what your action plan is. If we use weight control as an

illustration, you might have written down such things as, "I will run a mile every day." "I will eat three balanced meals per day." "I will ingest only 1,500 calories per day." The action plan should be specific to attaining the goal.

5. *Implement your action plan.* Too many times, individuals develop action plans but never implement them. There is no result or benefit without implementation, so it is critical and vital to implement the plan. Design a systematic time table to accomplish each phase of your action plan.

6. *Evaluate your plan.* During the evaluation phase you will discover the following: (1) that you reached your goal because your action plan was appropriate and you took action or, (2) you did not reach your goal because your action plan was faulty or, (3) you did not reach your goal because you did not implement your action plan. Once you analyze your situation you are in a position to make the following decisions:

   a) Pat yourself on the back and improve your self-image because you have attained the goal.

   b) Rework your action plan so that it can be made to work.

   c) Implement your existing action plan so that you can get on with accomplishing your goals.

7. *Feedback.* The information you gained during your evaluation should be used as input at the beginning of the goal-setting system to keep the process ongoing until you reach your goal.

As you can see, there are seven steps to the goal-setting model. Let's review them one more time.
1. Identify your vision, dream, or want.
2. State your goal.
3. List all benefits.
4. Describe your action plan.
5. Implement your action plan.
6. Evaluate your plan.
7. Feedback.

I am now going to share an idea with you that will allow you to determine prior to implementing your action plan whether or not you will be successful when and if you do. All you need to do is to compare your list of benefits to your action plan. This will give you a quick visualization of whether or not you are serious about carrying out the action plan so that you can achieve the goal. In fact, what it does is the following:

The list of benefits are the rewards you will attain by achieving the goal.

Your action plan is the price you will have to pay to attain the benefits.

When you compare these two items, the question you need to ask is, "Is it worth the time, energy, money and resources that the action plan will require to attain the benefits that will result?" If your answer is a clear, decisive, positive "yes," your chances of achieving the goal are exceptionally high. On the other hand,

Goal-Setting

if your response is to hesitate, to not be sure, then your chances are reciprocal and you can count on not achieving the goal. When this occurs, it indicates that your vision, dream or want is not something that is of paramount importance to you. Usually when individuals have a burning desire to achieve a goal, they will proceed to do whatever needs to be done to accomplish that particular goal. Hence, I cannot over-exaggerate the need for you to take time out to identify what your true visions, dreams and wants are in your life. Once this is identified, the goal-setting formula works extremely well. The motivational level of the individual is extremely high and the energy output from the individual to attain the goal is inexhaustible.

Another key concept in goal-setting is something I call "controllable goal-setting." The primary function of controllable goal-setting is to set goals over which you have total control. This guarantees you will have success. Let me illustrate.

Foot in the Door

If my goal is to take my wife out to dinner, that becomes uncontrollable because when I ask my wife out to dinner, she may say "no." Hence, I would not have achieved my goal. This would produce negative reinforcement and an attitude in me that goal-setting may or may not work. However, if I set the goal in controllable terms, I can have total control over the situation. For example, instead of saying "I will take my wife out to dinner," I would say "I will invite my wife out to dinner." Hence, I have total control and, therefore, no negative reinforcement. It also reinforces the concept that goal-setting works.

You can apply the idea of controllable goal-setting to controllable action plans. For example, when you develop your action plans to achieve your goals, wherever possible set plans that you have control over. When you have to depend on other people, your chances of achieving the goal become less. This is not to say that in achieving many of your goals you will not have to depend on people, for, in fact, you will. However, where you do not need to do this, don't! Where you do have to depend on people, remember: the key individual that you need to depend on most is yourself!

At this point, an illustration of how the goal-setting formula works with a specific example might be helpful. Let's assume Mary Jones would like to lose 30 pounds. Let's take Part I of the formula.

What might her vision or dream or want be? Well, it might be that she would look trim and slim so that other people would praise her. Or that she would feel better about herself because she could fit into a smaller dress or slack size. Finally, she might see her improved figure in a mirror and feel better about herself which, in fact, would improve her self-image. In any event, Mary Jones needs a vision. In this case, let's say that her vision is to be able to wear a certain size dress to a wedding that will be taking place in the spring and, at this wedding, she will meet many of her friends who will, in fact, praise her for the way she looks — thirty pounds less. Her goal would be to lose 30 pounds by the time of the wedding. She would be specific; she would write it down; she would put a date on it; she would look at it every day; she would repeat it; she might share it with her husband or a friend. The benefits for losing the weight would be to improve her self-image, to be healthier, to be able to buy clothes in a smaller size, to increase her confidence and to look better. Her action plan could be to reduce her intake by 500 calories per day, increase her physical activity level, and eat three balanced meals per day. She would implement her plan and evaluate it when she was through. Information from the evaluation would be used as feedback to motivate her onward toward her goal.

Mary definitely can attain her goal if she chooses. In order for this to occur, she will have to really want it and be willing to pay the price. As you look at your own life, have there not been goals you have wanted to achieve but have been unwilling to pay the price, or, is it possible that you have not identified clearly the visions, dreams and wants that you desire? Remember, it is at this stage that the energy and drive develops to move you towards the completion of your goals. Do positive thinking and goal-setting assure instant success? No, not at all. Even if you are following the formula precisely, there is no 100 percent guarantee for success. Look at it this way. Every successful person has had to deal with failures and cope with setbacks. Such individuals perceive the failure, setback, and disappointment as only a slight detour. They realize they can grow from each failure. It is this very growth during failure that eventually will make them a success. Remember the orginal formula of a **Self-Powered Person**. K plus A equals BB. That's you.

There are two other aspects of goal-setting which may need further clarification. The first has to do with failure. Do you know the feeling? You goofed; you messed up; you bombed. **Self-Power** says that's okay. That's the human dimension. No one is perfect. When someone takes an action, isn't that better than another person's not acting at all? Growth comes from action. That's the key and you have the power to turn the key.

Just one word of caution about handling a flop. It's not a particularly opportune time to introduce a large dose of constructive criticism. A **Self-Powered Person** handles failures by seeing the growth potential in all situations. Remember, you do control what you look for in each situation. You have the power to use it as a stumbling block or a building block. The choice is yours.

There is one other aspect of goal-setting to consider. Goal-setting is not to be confused with wishful thinking. A goal is not a pie-in-the-sky idea. Remember, the key to positive thinking is to activate simple, concrete plans. There is a process, a series of intermediate steps, a progression toward attaining a goal. That's something different from wishing on a star.

The questions are: WHAT ARE YOUR LIMITS? HOW DO YOU KNOW? Everyone who wants to be a **Self-Powered Person** has to wrestle with these questions. You must think positively and be prepared to do the best with what you have. Let's not get caught up setting limitations for ourselves and others. Stop telling yourself and others they can't. Let's foster positive growth. When we choose to do this we will be happier and more productive.

The refrain has grown familiar. Again, **Self-Power** acknowledges that you can grow personally. You have the **Self-Power** to change. You can be in control of your life and the manner in which you react to events in your life. You can interact with people in a positive way, see the potential for growth, even in negative events. You have the capacity to establish realistic, concrete goals. This may sound a bit like Utopia and it might be, except for the fact that **Self-Power Concepts** work if you work **Self-Power Concepts**.

A Self-Power Positive Action Plan:

Implement the positive action plan that follows:

This activity will help you establish and realize concrete, attainable goals.

1. For the next week avoid the word "can't." Substitute the

word "can" in your daily vocabulary.
2. Avoid the use of the phrase "I will try." Utilize the concept "I will."
3. Instead of saying "I have to," use the thought, "I've decided to."
4. Focus your attention and energies on establishing simple, concrete attainable goals.
5. Make a list of 5 important goals you really want to attain. For each goal, identify the benefits that would accrue when you achieved that goal.

Summarizing Self-Power Concepts Thus Far

Self-Power acknowledges that you can grow. You have the self-power to change. You can be in total control of your life and the way in which you react to unforeseen events in your life. You can interact with people in a positive way, see the potential for growth even in negative events. You have the ability to establish concrete goals and the potential to achieve them.

A Self-Power Activity

Title: PERSONAL INVENTORY

This activity provides you with additional insights into your potential strengths and weaknesses. Answer each question in terms of how you see yourself at the present time.

1. Do you daydream about some special goal in life not yet achieved?_____

Goal-Setting

2. If so, do you visualize yourself achieving the goal? How?_____

3. Would you describe yourself as a goal-achieving individual or a self-limiting personality?_____

4. What do you consider to be your greatest strengths and weaknesses?

   My Greatest Strengths_____

   My Greatest Weaknesses_____

5. What attributes do you need to acquire in order to grow personally and/or professionally?_____

Foot in the Door

6. Do you consider yourself to be a lucky or unlucky person?____

7. Do you feel there are still a lot of things you would like to do in your lifetime?____

8. Are the choices in your life limited or unlimited?

9. What are the major factors that influence your life?

10. How can you achieve greater self-direction?____

Summarize what you have learned about yourself by having completed this personal inventory. Then write down what you plan on doing to put yourself into a positive growth pattern. Do it.

____
____
____
____
____
____

Goal-Setting

Chapter VI

Failure Will Lead to Success If You Allow It

A critical notion one needs to deal with as it relates to failure is simply this: Those who are successful are individuals who have failed numerous times. This is consistent with anyone you speak to who is successful.

Let's examine the process a little more closely. Individuals who never fail probably never try. Hence, there is no failure and no personal and professional growth. The reciprocal of this is that individuals who are successful have indeed failed. However, the critical difference is this: Those who are successful have learned that when they fail, they can learn from their failure to produce future successes. Hence, when failure occurs, they seek out growth opportunities to move them in a forward direction for the future.

Another striking characteristic of successful people is that they do not fear failure. They concentrate on the goal and believe before they achieve the goal that they will be successful. This thinking process allows them to achieve goals that failures never do.

Even when one sets a goal, implements an action plan and, in fact, does not achieve the particular goal, that individual has grown. Although the individual did not hit the mark, he or she still has grown, and this will lead to future successes which again will help develop potential.

If you would like to test this idea, try this experiment. Talk to someone who is extremely successful. Ask him if he's ever failed. I can assure you that he will say yes, many times. Then, talk to someone you know who you do not believe to be very successful and ask if he has ever failed. Most times unsuccessful people will tell you that they really haven't failed that often.

Isn't it better to fail and grow than never to try and just get by? What do you think? The most significant stumbling block in the failure attitude is that individuals are afraid of feeling bad as a result of failing. For example, when an individual fails at something people may laugh and criticize that person. Such criticism usually makes the person feel bad. Thus, you learn early in life that when you fail you also will feel bad. In order to protect yourself you begin to be very careful of the risks you take because you don't want to feel bad. This kind of thinking leads to atrophied personal and professional growth. You can change this kind of thinking by examining the process more carefully and recognizing that it is in your best interest to risk and not to worry about failure.

Let me illustrate my point with the following example: You watched your friend or business associate set a goal and work extremely hard to achieve it, but in the end that person did not reach the goal. What would your perception of him be? I would think you would respect and admire him because he went for it. He set a goal, developed a plan, implemented it, and was willing to take a risk. Terrific. That's what we should all be doing, setting goals and going for them. I admire people like that. How about you? If you are willing to admire *them* for setting goals and going for them even when they fail, it makes good sense that you and I should do the same thing. When you choose to think this way you will not fear the bad feelings associated with failure. Instead you will release energy and drive in your system which will assist you in achieving your goals. **Absolutely Fantastic.**

Following is a check list of characteristics associated with the failure-prone personality. I would recommend that you check those characteristics you believe you possess. Be honest with yourself. After completing this task, develop and implement specific action plans to reduce and eliminate your personal failure characteristics.

Don't be afraid of this activity. It can be very enlightening and a beginning toward a self-image of success rather than failure. You will definitely grow from this activity.

FAILURE CHARACTERISTICS CHECKLIST

Failure Characteristics	Check Those You Possess	Action Plan to Minimize & Eliminate Failure Characteristics
The Failure:		
1. Fears Failure		
2. Blames others for lack of success		
3. Is uncooperative		
4. Talks down to people		
5. Has no plan		
6. Procrastinates		
7. Has no written goal		
8. Does not believe		
9. Doesn't take time to be successful		
10. Does not read and listen		
11. Pre-judges		
12. Is not prepared		
13. Dwells on problems		
14. Can't accept the success of others		
15. Sees the negative in everything		
16. Doesn't tell it like it is		

*Use additional paper where necessary.

Self-Powered Persons identify the goal, develop and implement the plan, and believe they will succeed. Finally, the **Self-Powered Person** recognizes that in failure there is growth and in growth there is opportunity for success and happiness.

Summary

Is failure good or bad? As you can see, it is definitely good if your thinking is correct. You grow from failure. The activities in this chapter were designed to illustrate the misconception that one should fear failure. Go for the things you want in life and you will be excited about life. When you fail, learn from your failures and pat yourself on the back for having the guts and positive self-image to go for it. When you do this, you will be a leader of yourself as well as others.

Chapter VII

Dealing with Stress as a Positive and Productive Force in Your Life

It is difficult to think of a topic about which more has been written than the subject of stress, for as the complexities of life have increased in our nuclear society, so, too, has stress. Yet stress is a part of life and, since one cannot eliminate it, one must learn to deal with it successfully.

In order to deal effectively with stress, it is necessary to understand the mechanism of stress and the physiological response stress produces within the body.

One of the leading proponents of stress management is the noted author and researcher Hans Selye. In his research he describes three phases in the stress response. Selye called this

Foot in the Door

process the General Adaptation Syndrome. Selye describes the first stage of the General Adaptation Syndrome as the ALARM phase. The ALARM phase is the initial shock phase. Some call it the *fight or flight* stage. If you were accosted by a mugger, would you fight or flee? In response to such a stressor the body will prepare to fight or flee. It should be noted that the same physiological reaction will occur even though there may or may not be physical danger to the individual. The stressor also could be psychological, which would trigger the alarm reaction. Examples of stressors that could trigger the ALARM phase are:

a) Giving a speech

b) Being chased by an animal

c) Being followed late at night

d) A promotion on your job

e) Participating in an athletic event

f) Receiving a telegram

g) Getting a pink slip at work

The second phase of the General Adaptation Syndrome is called the RESISTANCE phase, which is the chemical rallying of the body's defenses to help the body get back to homeostasis or equilibrium. During this phase the individual may be tense, have elevated blood pressure, increased heart rate, and ultimately have a depletion of energy. When the RESISTANCE phase is permitted to continue it will lead to the third stage, which is the EXHAUSTION phase. This is the final stage of the stress response. It is characterized by an increase in somatic complaints such as headaches, ulcers, tightness in the stomach, and an array of other physical and mental disorders. Following is a diagram of the General Adaptation Syndrome.

General Adaptation Syndrome

```
              RESISTANCE
         ┌─────────────────┐
     ALARM│ MIND & BODY   │ EXHAUSTION
    /STRESSOR-│ WORKING   │DISEASE\
   /PSYCHOLOGICAL│ TOGETHER │OCCURS \
  / OR PHYSICAL │ TO DEAL  │        \
 /              │ WITH     │         \
/               │ STRESSOR │          \
```

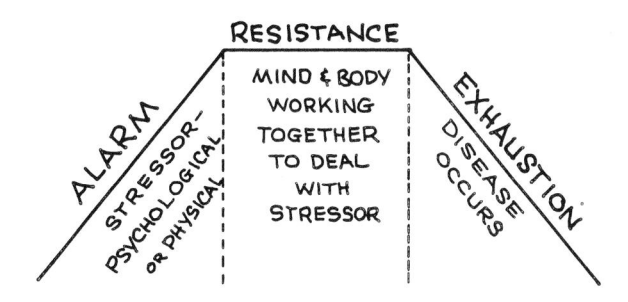

Many parallels can be drawn between the onset of illness and the level of stress. Some illnesses have an insidious onset. They occur gradually over a period of time. It is difficult to pinpoint the exact time or way the illness began. Even the patient is unaware of the onset. So, too, with stress. It has an accumulative effect. Unresolved stress leads to more stress rather than remaining constant or diminishing. The amount of stress in one's life increases and eventually produces a negative effect. It's important, therefore, to be in tune with one's stress level, to recognize the signs of stress for you personally and to learn how to develop an action plan to deal with stress effectively.

To eliminate stress from your life is not the goal. First of all, that's impossible. Secondly, the physiological response known as the fight or flight response is a necessary survival skill. Thirdly, stress is positive. It is only when the level of stress becomes so

Foot in the Door

high that is no longer stress but actually *distress* that we are in trouble. It might be easier to visualize stress/distress zones in one's life by the following diagram:

Stress Curve

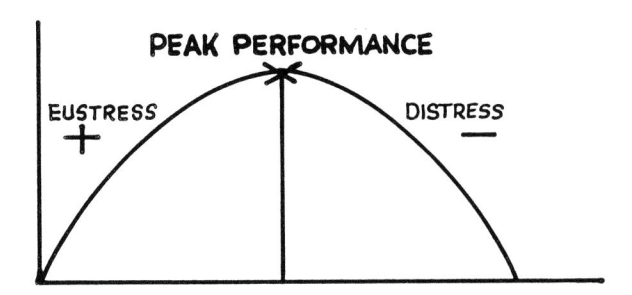

```
              PEAK PERFORMANCE
                    ✕
    EUSTRESS    │        DISTRESS
       +        │            ─
```

This linear drawing illustrates that the level of stress constantly changes. There are safe levels within which the individual functions adequately and copes intelligently with stressors. In fact, while an individual is on the left side of the scale, stress is a positive force. For example, the schoolboy who has to recite a paper in front of the class, the mother who is preparing Thanksgiving dinner for the entire family, and the baseball player who is preparing to take his place at the plate. All of these individuals are experiencing stress. So long as their stress level is on the left side of the curve, which we call Eustress, it will assist them in performing well. We must be cognizant, however, of the signs of Distress.

There are three categories of distress with which you should become familiar. They are MOOD, VISCERAL, and MUSCULOSKELETAL.

First, your Mood. *Signs to look for:*

> Worry
> Nervousness
> Over-excitability
> Insecurity
> Being ill at ease
> Personal discomfort

Second, your Visceral. *Signs to look for:*

> Cold chills
> Feeling faint
> Dry mouth
> Upset stomach
> Loss of appetite
> Headaches
> Heart palpitations
> Flushing of the face and neck

Third, your Musculoskeletal. *Signs to look for:*

> Muscle twitching
> Trembling of fingers and hands
> Muscle tension or tightness
> Stuttering
> Difficulty in fine motor movements

When you have any combination of these signs, you can be assured that something is going on in your life that is producing stress. At such times, it is important for you to act appropriately and decisively so that you can move from the Distress side back to the Eustress side of the stress curve. Remember, you will be more effective and healthier when you are on the *eustress* side of the curve. You can learn to do this by controlling your thinking processes and being a **Self-Powered Person**.

Practical Solutions To Effective Stress Management

To cope successfully with stress there are four basic rules. They are easy to learn, but somewhat more difficult to practice in a consistent manner. Let's take one rule at a time.

The first rule is to RECOGNIZE THAT YOU ARE UNDER DISTRESS. Don't deny its existence or its impact on your mood or behavior. That means you admit there are persons in your life who are potential stressors for you. There are situations which you know clearly cause you stress. From your knowledge of signs and symptoms of distress you should be able to recognize when you are under distress. The major point of this rule is to become aware of your distress level so you can do something actively about it.

The second rule is to IDENTIFY THE ETIOLOGY/CAUSE OF THE DISTRESS. Usually the cause of the distress is your reaction to events that involve people. We will discuss this concept in more detail later in this chapter.

The third rule is to DEVELOP A POSITIVE ACTION PLAN TO REDUCE OR ELIMINATE THE DISTRESS. This can best be accomplished by thinking of things you can do to help the situation. When you need the assistance of others ask them for their help. The key point is to write the action plan down and then get on with it.

The fourth rule is to WRITE DOWN THE DATE THAT YOU WILL BEGIN IMPLEMENTING YOUR POSITIVE ACTION PLAN. Actually write the date down. There is something about writing things down that helps people. What did you learn from this activity? Be specific._____

_____
_____
_____
_____
_____
_____
_____
_____
_____

As you begin to use these steps you will be able to identify the problem and organize your resources more effectively. This will lead you to positive adaptation and ultimately a solution. Researchers in stress management have discovered that individuals who actively pursue solving stress problems invariably reduce their stress levels just by the mere fact that they are doing something actively about it. Hence, it is critical to get involved with dealing actively with the stressors in your life. You can do it.

Your Thinking as It Relates to Stress

As one studies the area of stress, it becomes increasingly clear that the individual is the key element in dealing with stress. While there are many descriptions of the stress response, there are few that emphasize the strong relationship between stress and the mind. In the following paragraphs I would like to describe an expanded point of view as to how one should perceive stress.

Let's begin by defining stress as visualizing failure or events negatively. This definition is simple, yet potent. Let's test the definition. Think of a situation where you are under tremendous stress. Analyze that situation and ask yourself this question: Weren't you really under stress because you were visualizing failure or you thought there would be a negative outcome? Think about it. This is typically the situation. One perceives that something is going to go wrong and this, in turn, produces stress.

Let me use another illustration to highlight this point. Have you ever heard an individual say, "Hit that person's hot button and you can get him to produce." This is true only in a positive sense. You can also hit the hot button of people in the negative sense which, in turn, will produce tremendous stress. The key question, then, is can we teach ourselves how to hit our hot buttons positively and minimize and control the hitting of our negative hot buttons? The answer to both parts of this question is yes. Let me explain.

When someone hits your hot button, that person typically has produced an image in your mind that causes you to respond in a positive sense. For example, if someone starts talking to you about a vacation in Hawaii in the middle of January, you might start to get all sorts of warm feelings and images of being in Hawaii. This in turn might result in your getting excited about a possible trip, making plans for the trip, and thinking of ways to earn extra income so you can afford the trip.

On the other hand, if someone brings up a situation where you have failed, lost your job, didn't pass the test, or didn't lose enough weight, you may begin to create negative pictures in your mind which will definitely produce tension and stress.

In both situations the key elements are the images that you produce in your mind. When the images are positive, you feel good and have energy and drive. When the images are negative, you will experience high distress levels and feel bad. The key to the process is the way you think.

Question: Is it possible for someone to create a negative situation that deals with failure and for you to be able to control your thinking so you do not create distress in your life? The answer is definitely yes.

The most effective way to do this is to follow the positive thinking model which was described in Chapter III. As you review the material on positive thinking you will discover that it produces positive pictures in your mind which reduce and eliminate distress.

Before I explain another process for controlling stress, you and I need to recognize that no one else produces distress in our lives. *We produce the distress. To put it another way, it is our reaction to the stimuli coming into our minds that makes the difference. We must remember that we have little or no control over events in our lives, but total control over how we react to these events.*

Pelizza's Model for Effective Stress Management

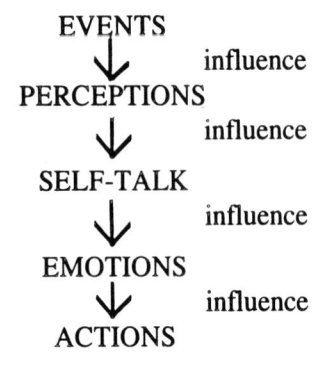

$$
\begin{array}{c}
\text{EVENTS} \\
\downarrow \quad \text{influence} \\
\text{PERCEPTIONS} \\
\downarrow \quad \text{influence} \\
\text{SELF-TALK} \\
\downarrow \quad \text{influence} \\
\text{EMOTIONS} \\
\downarrow \quad \text{influence} \\
\text{ACTIONS}
\end{array}
$$

Events are those things that you and I are experiencing. For example, let's assume that you just received a pink slip at work and were told your job would be terminated in two weeks. This is the event. This event has the power to influence your perception. Which would it be? I am going to lose my job and therefore I am not worth anything; I will not be able to feed my family; I always knew I would be a failure; *or*, now I need to get on with finding a job that I really like and one that will help me grow. What are the possibilities that I could be trained for another job in the company? What are my alternatives? Remember, you control your thinking. Your perception will influence your self-talk. If you say, I am a bad person because I am going to lose my job, or I am a failure, or I will never find another job because I am too old, your self-talk will generate negative emotions in you. You would probably get angry and depressed if you continued to use negative self-talk and thus, not find another job. However, if you choose to use positive self-talk you would increase your probability of finding another job. Finally, your emotions will move you into positive action, negative action, or no action. The key to this process is your perception, which is how you think and interpret stimuli in your environment and the self-talk that you allow yourself to repeat. It should be obvious to you that positive thinking and positive self-talk are preferable to negative. What I like most about this process is that you and I can choose which way to think. Isn't that fantastic?

Once you realize that distress really evolves from your perceptions and self-talk you are in a position to take control. The next time you are experiencing distress ask yourself: What am I thinking about? What kind of self-talk am I repeating to myself? I can assure you that it is negative. Change it to positive and you will be able to begin to effectively manage your stress level. This model is easy to follow and, most important, it works. After you use it several times you will feel terrific because you will have a sense of control. Follow it. It will make you feel better.

Foot in the Door

Practical Ways to Reduce Stress

The following list of activities is designed to help you reduce the stress in your life. It is also designed to allow you to participate in activities that will assist you in becoming a **Self-Powered Person**. Select those activities which are appropriate for you and then take action. The more of these activities you participate in on a regular basis, the greater your control will be over your stress level. Here they are:

Walk fifteen minutes to one hour per day. This should be vigorous walking. Wear proper footwear to give your feet support.

Jog three to five times per week. According to Dr. Kenneth Cooper, jogging 15 miles per week will result in cardiovascular improvement. Wear proper jogging attire.

Dealing with Stress

Participate in a recreational activity that you can get lost in, such as a craft, painting, woodworking, bicycling, tennis, swimming, golf, racquetball or gardening. I'm sure you can think of others. The way you will know that you have a good recreational activity is that you will lose track of time when you are involved with it.

Spend time in total quiet every day — approximately 5-15 minutes per day. This will allow your system to replenish itself with energy. During this time think pleasant thoughts or no thoughts at all.

Deal with the present and not the past. We can all handle one day at a time. We get into trouble when we add in yesterdays and tomorrows. Remember, the past is gone; the future has not yet arrived; what you have is NOW, so concentrate on it.

Be able to recognize stress in your life and take action to deal with it. Stress has the potential to turn you on, get you going, or it can stop you dead in your tracks. Your thinking will determine which one.

Accept the fact that life includes a certain amount of inevitable frustration. You can deal with and accept frustration because it is going to help you grow.

Enjoy little things every day: A smile from a friend, a sunset, a good cup of coffee. At the end of the day concentrate on all the good things that you have experienced. This will make you feel good.

Give help to others. When you give help to others you feel good right away and so do they. Everyone wins.

Strive for self-fulfillment at every stage of the life cycle. There is excitement and change at every stage if you look for it. It's worth looking for.

Talk it out. Share what is inside of you with someone you trust. It will make you feel better and help develop and maintain a relationship.

Don't be accountable for things you have no control over. Be totally accountable for those things you do have control over, like your thinking.

Do the very best you can with what you have. You can't ask more of yourself than that, can you?

Give yourself positive self-talk every day. It will improve your self-image and make you feel good.

Learn to listen to your body talk. Become aware of your mental and physical well-being, and when it gets out of balance do something actively to correct it.

Balance work with play. When you balance both of these you will become synergistic.

Avoid relying on alcohol and drugs to help you cope. Deal head-on with the events in your life. Don't cover them up with alcohol and drugs.

Avoid loneliness. Get involved with people, animals, and nature.

Get enough rest and sleep on a regular basis. Find out what is appropriate for you and make sure you work it into your routine.

Be thankful for what you have and not for what you have just lost. This idea will get you through the tough times. It really works.

Remember, **Knowledge Plus Action Equals Big Benefits. Take the Action.**

Write down the Key Ideas you have learned about stress management. For each idea write down a positive action you can take to put yourself into a positive growth pattern.

_____
_____
_____
_____
_____
_____
_____
_____
_____
_____
_____
_____
_____
_____
_____

Chapter VIII

How to Use Your Creative Imagination for Personal and Professional Growth

In this chapter we will be discussing the power of your mind and how you can control the imprinting process in your mind so that you can grow in the areas you choose.

During the past two decades, a great deal of research has been conducted in terms of how the mind really works for personal and professional growth. The processes I will be describing in this chapter are known to few; however, most people have gone through these processes without knowing it. By understanding how these processes work, you will be in a position to utilize your mind more effectively so that you can move in a desired direction. Let us begin by examining how your mind works.

First, you have a conscious mind. Your conscious mind carries out a number of functions. For example: (1) it perceives events in the environment: (2) it associates these events with what has occurred in the past: (3) it evaluates these events based on the associations in the past: (4) it makes decisions based on the evaluation.

Hence, the conscious mind is that part of the mind that interacts with the environment so that you know what's going on. This part of the mind utilizes all of the senses that you possess so that you can maintain some degree of equilibrium in the environment.

A second process in the mind is called the subconscious. The primary purpose of the subconscious mind is recording. It's like a computer. When you think about something or give something thought, this is recorded in your subconscious mind. However, as time passes, many of these items which are in fact recorded in your subconscious mind are difficult to bring to the surface and utilize. An important point to recognize is that the subconscious mind records what one thinks about. Hence, there is a great deal of data stored in the subconscious mind which in fact will determine many of your future behaviors and perceptions based on associations from the conscious mind to the subconscious mind. Let me illustrate.

If, on numerous occasions, you have spoken in front of a group and became nervous, perspired, and stuttered, each time this

Foot in the Door

event occured it would be recorded in your subconscious mind. Now, if the opportunity presents itself for you to speak before a group of people, what does your mind do?

1. It perceives the situation at the conscious level and sees that there are people around who will be listening to you.
2. It associates at the conscious level by drawing on the data stored in the subconscious mind. What does it find? It finds that in the past when you spoke in front of groups you perspired, became tense, and stuttered. Now your conscious mind evaluates the situation and says, "Wow! Should I do this again?" When you must decide, your answer will most likely be "No" because you don't wish to go through such a traumatic experience.

Thus, the conscious mind and the subconscious mind interact with each other in order to allow the organism to function well. In many cases, however, because negative data has been stored in the subconscious mind it will restrict your actions. It is in the subconscious mind that we can use a process known as Creative Imagination to imprint positive data so that when the conscious mind associates the data in the subconscious mind, it will support the actions you know you need to take in order to move in a desired direction.

Let me illustrate this. If we were able, and we can do this, to imprint a positive image in your subconscious mind as it relates to speaking in front of a group, then the next time you are in that situation your conscious mind will go into your subconscious data bank and come back with data that says, "Speaking in front of people is enjoyable; it makes me feel good and worthwhile." Hence, your decision will most likely be to speak in front of the group. So, how do we go about imprinting into the subconscious mind positive data?

Before we get into the specifics of the imprinting process, let me make a few points about Creative Imagination. In the past, when high performance people have been interviewed and examined as to why they performed so much better than other people, it became increasingly clear that one characteristic they all possessed was that they used their Creative Imagination to see themselves functioning well in situations prior to the situation occurring. For example, high performance people in the arts, athletics, politics, business, and religion will tell you that they vividly see themselves functioning well prior to the event. If we examine this process more closely, what we find is that such individuals rehearse the activity in their minds prior to its actually occurring. What this does in effect is put a piece of positive data in the subconscious mind which then in turn becomes the reality of that individual. Thus, when individuals perceive a situation such as speaking in front of people and refer to the subconscious data bank, they find that via constructive imagination they have had positive experiences with such situations. Therefore, they are motivated to go ahead and speak in front of groups.

A term we often use to describe this process is called **Self-Talk.** Self-Talk is nothing more than what you say to yourself. It can be a very positive force in your life or it can be quite destructive. For example, when a typist is typing a letter and makes an error and repeats to herself under her breath or just in her mind, "That's just like me to make an error!", what she has done in effect is to have imprinted in her subconscious mind that she makes errors, that this is just like her. So, in time, she will continue to make errors because this is her reality structure; it is just like her; it is normal. This can be changed by programming into her subconscious mind that she does not make errors when she is typing letters. This **Self-Talk Process** is one that people should undertake every day. What is unfortunate is that most people are very willing to give themselves a great deal of negative Self-Talk, which then comes to pass. I will, therefore, urge you never to talk negatively to yourself. This is negative Self-Talk and is destructive.

He talks to his "self" every day, an' he's beginning to make sense.

The reciprocal of this is also true. I strongly encourage you to provide yourself with a great deal of positive **Self-Talk** every day. This will reinforce the positive actions you want to be taking so that you can move in the direction you choose to move.

Another way to look at the process of **Self-Talk** is to refer to the Self-Talk Scale.

Self-Talk Scale

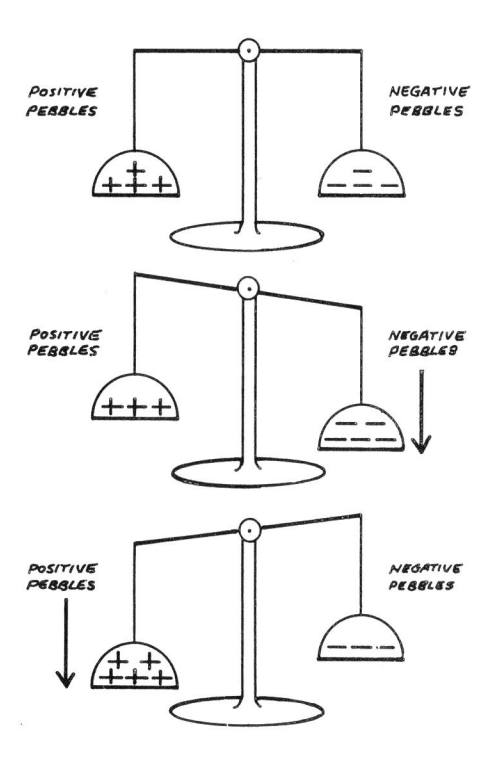

On one side of the scale are what we call "positive pebbles" and on the other side of the scale are "negative pebbles." Each time you provide yourself with positive or negative **Self-Talk**, what you are doing in effect is placing either a positive or negative "pebble" on the scale. Whichever side of the scale has the greater degree of positive or negative "pebbles" is the way you will act.

Foot in the Door

A key point to state at this time is this: Your present thoughts determine your future. Let me say it another way: What you think about is what you do and become. Hence, if you are continually placing negative "pebbles" on your scale, this is the way you will act. The opposite is also true. If you place positive "pebbles" on the scale, this will be the way you will behave. Therefore, it is to your advantage to be using **Self-Talk** positively so that you have many positive "pebbles" on the scale and thus will behave in a manner that is helpful and productive to you.

At this time I want to make an important statement. *You have total control over your self-talk and the number of pebbles you will be placing on your scale. You determine this process and it is important for you to accept this responsibility and use it wisely.*

Thus far in this chapter I have discussed the power of Creative Imagination, which is simply the process of vividly imagining an experience which has not yet taken place and which produces emotion in your system. The second area I have discussed is **Self-Talk** which, again, is the process of what you say to yourself and how it impacts on your future behavior. Put quite simply, positive **Self-Talk** produces positive results. Negative **Self-Talk** produces negative results.

The third area or process I want to discuss with you is the process of Affirmation. This process is designed to allow you at will to imprint positive data into your subconscious mind so that you can move in any direction you chooose. What, then, is an affirmation?

An affirmation is taking a future-oriented goal and putting it in the present tense, first person. Let me illustrate:

Let's say your goal was to become more self-confident. The way you would write an affirmation based on this goal would be: *I Am a Self-Confident Person.* What you are doing with this process is taking a future-oriented goal and putting it in the present tense just as though it already existed. What this does is imprint into the subconscious mind a positive "pebble" which, in fact, produces your reality or present thought structure, and as we said earlier, your present thought structure will determine your future actions.

Another way to look at affirmations is to refer to the Affirmation Model.

Affirmation Model

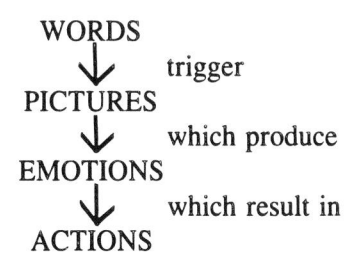

WORDS
↓   trigger
PICTURES
↓   which produce
EMOTIONS
↓   which result in
ACTIONS

As you can see in this model, words trigger pictures which produce emotion which, in effect, will result in action. Let me explain.

When you read a present-tense, first-person affirmation to yourself, what you are doing is imprinting into your subconscious mind this reality. When you read an affirmation, the words should allow you to see the picture of whatever it is you are affirming. For example, if your affirmation is to be a self-confident person, when you read this affirmation you should visualize and see pictures of what a self-confident person is. In your case, it may be standing in front of people and speaking or making a presentation to your boss or taking on added responsibilities at your job. It doesn't matter what it is. What does matter is that you see pictures of what self-confidence means to you.

The third step is that you experience emotion as a result of the pictures. When you get to the emotional level, when you feel it, the chances are very high that you will move into action so that you can attain the characteristic of the affirmation. In my opinion, the utilization of the affirmation process is one of the most powerful forces individuals can harness to assist themselves in attaining their goals.

Let me describe the affirmation process another way. An affirmation is a positive statement. It affirms that the goal has already come true. The theoretical basis of an affirmation is found in a sequence that relates words to mental pictures—something like creative imagination. For example, the word "vacation" evokes a picture of having fun, loafing, relaxing. The picture of you as a carefree individual evokes strong emotions such as the happy excitement of looking forward to a vacation. When this occurs, the emotion will move you into action so that you will do what needs to be done to accomplish the goal.

What I have just explained to you is an extraordinary concept. I can assure you that it works. It has worked for me personally and for many, many participants who have gone through my **Self-Power Concepts** seminars. Many of these participants have written to me or called me months later to describe the changes in their lives as a result of the affirmation process.

There is only one way to know for sure if the affirmation process works. You must do it. The following procedure should be followed in designing an affirmation program for yourself. Are you ready to begin? I hope so. It will change your life.

Organizing a Personal Affirmation Program

On the following six pages in this book you will find the following categories listed: Occupational, Recreational, Physical, Mental, Spiritual, and Social.

Do you remember this? These six categories are designed to give you balance. Hence, it makes sense, when you write affirmations, that you should have affirmations in each of these areas. This will give you balance and make you synergistic.

BALANCE IS IMPORTANT!

Under each of these six categories, list as many goals as you can think of that you would like to accomplish. It is important that you stop reading and do this activity. You will enjoy thinking about your goals. Once you have identified them, write them down. This will become the foundation of your affirmation program. Make sure the goals you write down are the ones you really want. The ones that turn you on. They will create an emotion in you.

Foot in the Door

OCCUPATIONAL GOALS

Write them down:

How to Use Your Creative Imagination

RECREATIONAL GOALS

Write them down:

Foot in the Door

PHYSICAL GOALS

Write them down:

MENTAL GOALS

Write them down:

_____
_____
_____
_____
_____
_____
_____
_____
_____
_____
_____
_____
_____
_____
_____
_____
_____
_____
_____
_____
_____
_____
_____

Foot in the Door

SPIRITUAL GOALS

Write them down:

SOCIAL GOALS

Write them down:

Foot in the Door

From this list of goals select two from each category that are most important to you. For each of these goals answer the following question in writing: *Why do I want it?* It is important that you write this information down.

WHY DO I WANT IT?

The second question you ask yourself is: *Why do I deserve these things?* Your response to this question is for all the goals you have set for yourself. Again, it is critical and imperative that you write down your response to this question.

WHY DO I DESERVE THESE THINGS?

Foot in the Door

The final question to which you need to react is: ***How does it feel now that I have these things?*** Let yourself feel the emotion. It will feel great. Your response to this question is imperative, and again, it should be written down.

HOW DOES IT FEEL NOW THAT I HAVE THESE THINGS?

The next step is to write an affirmation for each goal. Express the affirmation in the present tense, first person. Record each affirmation on a 3 x 5 card. You will utilize these cards to imprint the affirmation in your sub-conscious mind. Example:

I AM CONFIDENT

When is the best time to imprint the affirmation on your subconscious mind? Research clearly indicates that your subconscious mind is most receptive to imprinting the first thing in the morning when you rise from bed and the last thing you do before you go to bed. Hence, I will recommend that you read your affirmation as soon as you wake up in the morning, before you do anything else, and read your affirmation again just before going to bed. By reading your affirmation at these two times, you will imprint the goal in your subconscious mind. You may also read your affirmations during the day whenever you choose, but it's most important to read them in the morning and at night. The more frequently you read your affirmations, the sooner the process will work.

How long does it take for the affirmation process to work? Many people experience a change within the first week; however, to be realistic you should allow four to six weeks. At the end of this time you can go back and examine how the process has worked. I can assure you, you will have moved in a positive direction toward the affirmations you have been stating.

Some of your affirmations will already have come true. Others will be in the process of becoming true and you will be well aware of it. At this point you will totally believe in the affirmation process. You will also realize that you can continue to use this process for as long as you live so that you can continue to grow in whatever areas you choose. There are some other important points I want to mention about the affirmation process:

1. Your affirmations should always be positive. It is better to be moving toward something positive than away from something negative. **Example:** I don't lose my temper anymore. A better affirmation would be: I am an even-tempered person.

2. Be Categorical. Do not compare yourself with others in your affirmations. **Example:** I am the most productive teacher in my school. A better affirmation would be: I am an excellent teacher.

3. Express excitement. Interject words that cause you to become excited. **Example:** I weigh 175 pounds and feel fantastic! Or, I am proud of the fact that I am a dynamic public speaker. Such affirmations produce more emotion, which in turn will produce greater action.

4. Be Realistic. Do not develop affirmations that state perfection. **Example:** I organize my time perfectly. This is

unrealistic. It would be better to say: I am a well-organized person.

5. **Take Ownership.** Do not make the mistake of affirming for others. This is not possible. Affirmations are individualistic and only apply to the individuals who are imprinting them into their own minds. The purpose of affirmations is to affirm a change inside of *you*, not someone else. Remember, however, that when your attitude changes, the people around you usually change automatically. The simplest rule to follow in writing affirmations is to imagine that you have made the change you wish to make.

Learning to use affirmations effectively is perhaps the most difficult new skill that **Self-Powered Persons** have to master. It takes some practice, but don't get discouraged. I realize that you may have some doubt as to whether or not affirmations work and if, in fact, they are practical. I can assure you that (1) they work and (2) they are extremely practical.

As an additional aid, review the following affirmations which help to illustrate the process:

Notice that I have used the process of balance by writing two affirmations in each area. I would strongly suggest that, when you first begin the process, you have one or two affirmations in each area.

1. **Mental**
   It is easy for me to make difficult decisions on the job.

   I enjoy being a detail person.

2. **Physical**
   I look and feel great at 170 pounds.
   I am improving my cardiovascular endurance every day.
3. **Financial**
   It is easy for me to earn $100,000 each year.
   I enjoy writing to earn additional income.
4. **Social**
   It is easy for me to interact with people in new situations.
   I enjoy being well-dressed.
5. **Spiritual**
   I enjoy talking to God every day.
   I look forward to doing things for my church.
6. **Family**
   I enjoy meeting the needs of my wife.
   I love to spend time with my children.

One common affirmation that everyone should have is: I enjoy doing my affirmations. As usual, **Self-Power** wants the last word. In this case, it's another idea to help you grow personally and professionally. The reminder is, **Do it now!** T-N-T — Today, not tomorrow!

Write down the Key Ideas you have learned from this chapter on affirmations. For each idea write down a positive action you can take to put yourself into a positive growth pattern.

Chapter IX

A Self-Confidence Formula For You

Reduced to its simplest form, the Self-Confidence Formula is the "I can" rule. First, you must imagine in your mind that you are self-confident. Next, you must imagine whatever it is you want in your mind. Example: If you wanted to be an accomplished hostess, you would imagine yourself in this role. If you see yourself as a pilot, visualize yourself flying a plane.

Second, you must commit your energies to achieving this goal. The commitment to this effort is unconditional and non-negotiable. What this means is that there is no turning back. Quitting simply isn't permitted. Many people come close to attaining their goals, but just prior to accomplishing them they quit. Thus, commitment means you go for it until you exhaust all possibilities and personal energy.

Next, you use the Affirmation Process, which is to state and repeat the desired goal in the present tense, first person, as if the goal were already accomplished.

The fourth point is Never Give Up. Be persistent. It's possible that success may be almost in your grasp, so don't quit prematurely.

The four key actions are:

I — Imagine you are going to succeed
C — Commit yourself totally
A — Affirm your goal through affirmations
N — Never give up

As a final reminder, review the first letter of each word in vertical order. There it is: **I CAN**. Now you have it. There is no magic in the formula. The magic is in you.

Those who choose to use this formula can be guaranteed success in building their self-confidence. Once self-confidence is attained, it will guide you toward your goals. You should also recognize that one can always increase one's level of self-confidence. This is attained by becoming more than what you are and by accomplishing new and bigger goals. It's a never-ending process and an exciting one. I have always been impressed and stunned by the fact that those who are extremely successful always have a new set of goals they are working toward and they are the first to tell you that they are working on increasing their self-confidence level. One must therefore recognize that self-confidence is an ongoing process that allows you to become the person you are capable of becoming.

Self-Confidence Activity

Identify an area in which you would like to have more self-confidence. For example, speaking in front of groups. Commit your energies to achieving this goal; write an affirmation that affirms your having a high degree of self-confidence when you speak in front of groups; and, finally, continue to work toward this goal until you reach it.

A. Imagine. See yourself speaking successfully to a group of people. Draw a picture of this.

B. Commit. Write down what you are willing to do to achieve your goal.

_____
_____
_____
_____

C. Affirm. Write affirmations that will lead you toward reaching your goals.

_____
_____
_____
_____

D. Never Give Up. Write down key reasons why you will not quit as you pursue your goal.

_____
_____
_____
_____
_____

Allow four weeks for this type of concentrated activity and I assure you that you will see a difference in your self-confidence level. It will be much greater than it is now. You can do it.

Write down the Key Ideas you have learned about building your self-confidence level. For each idea write down a positive action you can take to put yourself into a positive growth pattern.

Chapter X

High Performance Characteristics of Self-Powered Individuals

During the past decade, a great deal of research has gone into analyzing what makes successful people tick. What is it about the highly successful individual that makes him different from those who never achieve high levels of success?

One astonishing fact that comes through clearly is that academic ability is not the key variable to one's success. This is not to say that academic ability is not important, because it is. However, there are other characteristics that play a more significant role in the success process. In this chapter I will share these characteristics with you so you can achieve high levels of success.

Other characteristics that have been associated with success are talent, hard work, intelligence, training, and experience. Although these characteristics play a role in helping an individual to become successful, they are not the most critical for success. This being true, and it is, we must ask: What are the true characteristics of high performance people? As each characteristic is identified and discussed, it should be made clear that **Self-Powered Persons** are those who seek to acquire and develop each of these characteristics to their fullest potential. The opposite is true of low or average performers. They have fewer of these characteristics and have little desire to work hard to acquire them.

High Performance Characteristics

1. *Self-Image*

    Self-Powered Persons have a high self-image. They see themselves as valuable, worthy and capable. They believe they stand for something good and know they can accomplish just about anything they set out to do. They feel they deserve success and are willing to pay the price to achieve it. They enthusiastically seek out new ways of achieving their goals and know they have control over the way they react to conditions which will lead them to success. In summary, they believe in themselves and know that if they put in the time and effort they will become whatever they want. Finally, they believe that their potential is unlimited.

2. *Accountability*

    Self-Powered Persons accept the results of their actions. They are willing to put themseves in motion and accept success as well as failure. They recognize that they may fail, but that much will be learned from these failures. They are able to recognize what causes success as well as failure. In either case they learn and grow, and continue to develop their potential. They make certain that they learn from their failures as well as reinforce the behaviors that produce success. In essence, they know where they are at any given point in time. They look for no excuses and continue to find ways to achieve their goals.

3. *Optimism*

   Self-Powered Persons look for good in everything they do. They believe that tomorrow will be a better day. They know that their actions of today will lead to future success. They are willing to invest time and talent in each day to move themselves toward a goal of tomorrow. They are individuals who are always looking for a solution to a problem when others are coming up with reasons why there is a problem. They are also fun people to be around.

4. *Goal-Oriented*

   Self-Powered Persons set goals continuously, visualize them, and continually work towards a goal. It is via this process that they get their energy and drive. Their behavior becomes automatic in doing what needs to be done in order to achieve their goals. Once the goal is reached a new goal is set to ensure continued energy and drive. The **Self-Powered Person** also has balance between personal, professional, group, and organizational goals.

5. *Imagination*

    Self-Powered Persons develop a pattern of focusing on positive contructive images toward which they want to move. They don't limit themselves by what has or has not been accomplished in the past but, rather, identify where they want to go, imagine themselves being there, and put energy and drive behind this imagination to achieve their goals. Research clearly indicates that people tend to move toward what they think about. Hence, the **Self-Powered Person** concentrates in areas such as job skills, cheerfulness, flexibility, healthy body, family harmony, love, spirituality, and happiness.

6. *Awareness*

    Self-Powered Persons are aware of their environment. They quickly identify information that will allow them to move toward the desired goal. They seize opportunities and act on them. They are constantly examining where they are and utilize every situation in which they become involved to move them toward their goal. This occurs because the individuals know where they are going and what needs to be done to get there. They are capable of picking up the signals in their environment which will allow them to achieve their goals.

7. *Creativeness*

    Self-Powered Persons are always ready to find new and better ways to achieve. Their minds continue to search for new ways and opportunities to approach problems. We know that all people have creativity. **Self-Powered Persons** use their creativity to their advantage. They develop this characteristic to a high degree of perfection and allow it to work for them spontaneously. They have also learned not to worry about what people say about their ideas, which may be different from the prevailing norm.

8. *Communication*

It is clear that success is largely rooted in your ability to get your ideas across and to understand what the other person is trying to communicate. **Self-Powered Persons** take full responsibility for making sure their message gets through in both directions. They are accountable for positive communications because they know that it is vital for them to understand what other people are saying.

9. *Personal and Professional Growth*

Self-Powered Persons recognize that they are in a constant state of growth both personally and professionally. They realize that they have the power to continually grow both personally and professionally when they are willing to expend time and energy for such growth. They also expect to grow.

10. *Positive Response To Stress*

    Self-Powered Persons use stress as a positive force in their lives. They recognize that living produces stress and that the ability to deal with stress effectively allows them to move in a positive direction. They use stress as a triggering mechanism to move and get into action. They welcome opportunities which put them under *eustress* so that they can demonstrate their effectiveness in this environment. They are also keenly aware of not allowing themselves to get into *distress*, which is a negative factor in productivity.

11. *Trust*

    Self-Powered Persons trust individuals. They believe that most people are good. They are willing to assist others in achieving their goals. They practice this philosophy in both their personal and professional lives. They value the trust others have in them and make sure they never abuse this trust.

12. *Joyfulness*

    Self-Powered Persons enjoy what they are doing; they are excited about moving toward a goal. They enjoy working and interacting with people. Through such interaction they continue to develop new energy and drive. This energy and drive radiates from them to those around them. It produces enthusiasm among the people with whom they interact.

13. **Risk-taking**

    Self-Powered Persons are willing to take risks. They realize that there are no guarantees, but that if one is willing to put effort into an area of interest, one has the capacity and potential to make things happen in one's favor. They also realize that if they fail they will learn from such failures so that they can continue to move ahead.

14. *Urgency*

    Self-Powered Persons have a sense of urgency about all the activities they participate in that are associated with reaching a goal. They want to get things done *now*. They make decisions *now* so that they can take action *now* in order to reach a desired goal. They enjoy making these decisions and don't look back on them. There is continuous excitement, intensity and joy in their daily living. They reflect a sense of power, motion, accomplishment and enthusiasm which becomes contagious to those around them. They also take time to rest and relax as they are achieving their goals.

15. *Happiness*

    Self-Powered Persons are happy individuals. They enjoy each day to the fullest. They identify and remember the positive things that occured during the day. Where something went wrong in their day they learn from it. They are constantly interacting and working with people. They have a lifetime goal of helping others achieve their goals. A **Self-Powered Person** is balanced, and a key characteristic of balance is a state of happiness.

Foot in the Door

Well, there you have it — fifteen characteristics of the **Self-Powered Person** — fifteen characteristics that have been identified in high performance people. How many of these characteristics do you possess? How many of these characteristics would you *like* to possess? Let me suggest the following: Where you possess the characteristics identified to some degree, improve on them. If you lack any of these characteristics, develop them. Develop affirmations for each characteristic so that you can develop them in your behavior. Develop them to the extent that they become automatic. Once you have developed these characteristics, your ability to develop your potential to its highest degree is within you. As a **Self-Powered Person** who contains these high performance characteristics, you will have the potential to achieve whatever it is you would like to achieve. But most important, *the goal that each of us is going for, the goal that is common to all of us, the one that we must have, is the goal of happiness.* Let us never forget that to achieve without happiness and joy is like preparing a scrumptuous dinner and having no one to serve it to or share it with.

The following activity is designed to assist you in acquiring the fifteen high performance characteristics of a **Self-Powered Person.** Put a check next to each high performance characteristic you possess. For those characteristics you do not possess, mark with a dash. For each dash you have, devise an action plan to acquire that characteristic. Your action plan should definitely include an affirmation for each characteristic. On a daily basis, ask yourself what you have done during the day to achieve that characteristic. Continue this process for at least a month. You will be amazed how many of these characteristics you can acquire within that short period of time. You also will be fascinated by the degree of **Self-Power** you will be demonstrating in both your personal and professional life. It will be an exciting venture. Most important, you will be on your way to becoming a happy individual.

Now that you have identified which high performance characteristics you need to work on, write them down in the space provided. Then write an affirmation for each one. Finally, use the affirmation process to help you acquire the high performance characteristics. I strongly encourage you to do this activity. It will make a big difference in your life. *You can do it.*

_____

_____

_____

_____

_____

_____

_____

_____

_____

_____

Chapter XI

Time Management

What is Time Management?

Time Management can be defined as follows:

It is your ability to use time effectively.

Each of us has 24 hours in a day. However, some individuals have the ability to utilize this time effectively so that they can grow personally and professionally in ways that seem difficult to others. On the other hand, there are individuals who never seem to have enough time and find themselves not becoming what they are capable of becoming. The critical difference when we examine both individuals is that the former is able to identify what he wants and utilizes the 24 hours in a day to his best advantage.

Time Management

A critical question for you to ask yourself is, are you using your time effectively? If not, why not?

Getting Started

To become more skillful in applying time management strategies to your personal and professional life you must first ask yourself why you want more time. Whatever the answer, it's up to you to make choices to make that want come true. The following procedure will help you do it.

Circle A represents how a typical person might allocate and spend his or her time in a typical day.

Circle A — Example:
The Way I Presently Spend My Time

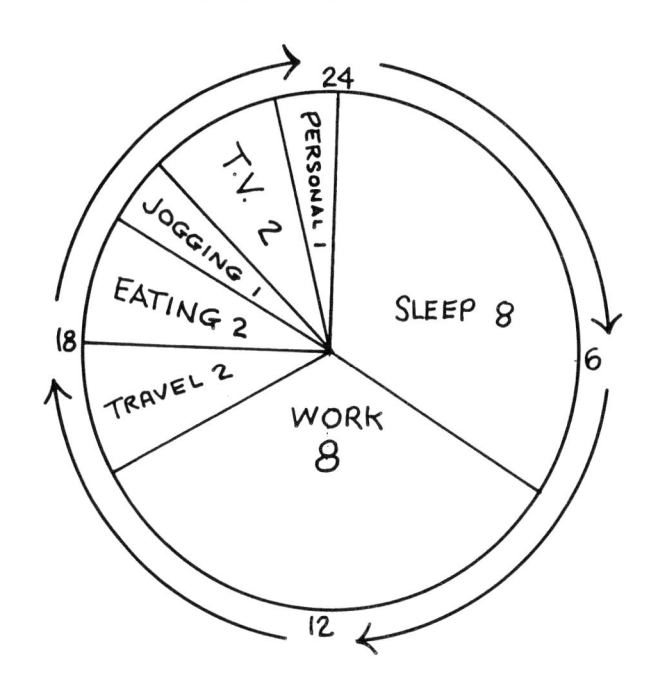

```
         24
      PERSONAL 1
    T.V. 2
  JOGGING 1
  EATING 2         SLEEP 8
18                          6
  TRAVEL 2
         WORK
          8
         12
```

Foot in the Door

Circle B is for you to carve out how you presently spend your time during a typical day. Be as specific as you can.

Circle B

The Way I Presently Spend My Time

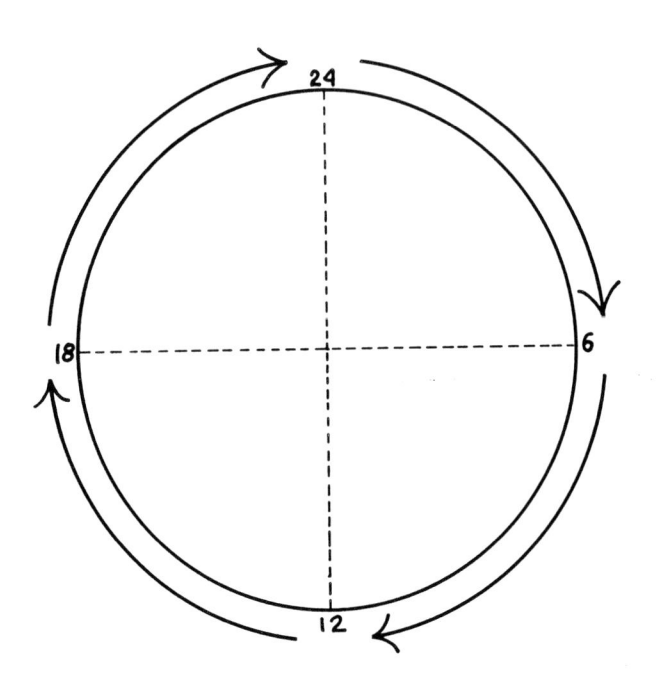

Next you need to decide how you should spend your time to be more effective and efficient. Repeat the procedure by completing Circle C, The Way I Want to Spend My Time. Be truthful.

Time Management

Circle C
The Way I Want To Spend My Time

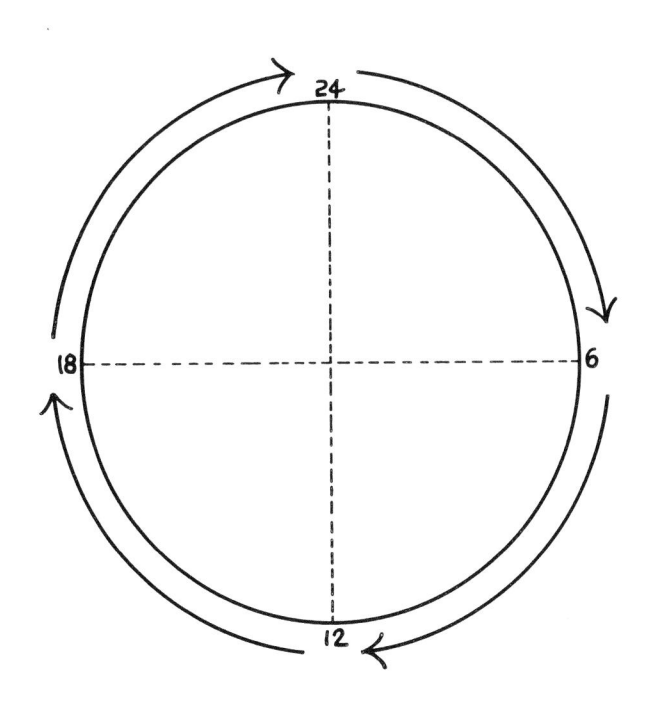

Study Circle C carefully. It should provide you with some important insights as to how you ought to be spending your time. Apply what you have learned from this activity. Do it soon. I would also suggest that you put Circle C in a place where you will see it every day. This will help you to take the appropriate actions. One more point: Look at Circle C and determine if you are spending enough time in the six areas that give a person balance. Those six areas, once again, are Occupational, Recreational, Physical, Mental, Spiritual, and Social. If you are out of balance, it is in your best interest to take action. Next I will present to you a variety of time management strategies that can help you get control of your time.

My Favorite
Time Management Strategies

The following time management strategies have been used over the past five years. These strategies have been shared in numerous seminars which I have presented and have been found to be extremely effective. I would, therefore, like to share these strategies with you and strongly suggest that you implement them. I can assure you that these time management strategies will assist you in getting control of your time and allowing you to achieve your goals in both your personal and professional life. Here they are:

1. Include in your daily schedule a period of time, approximately 15 minutes to one-half hour, to just relax and "get away from it all." When possible, use this time for walking. This strategy will allow you to clear your head, which will assist you in thinking clearly and, therefore, not making decisions which are incorrect. If you follow my suggestions on walking, it will assist you in burning calories and this will help you to maintain the proper weight. It will improve your muscle tone and, finally, help to dissipate anxiety and stress. All in all, this is an excellent strategy to follow.

2. Get your most unpleasant tasks out of the way first so that you are free to enjoy the balance of your day. This strategy is critical if you want to be moving in a positive direction on a daily basis. Let me explain. Too many people put the unpleasant tasks off until last. When you do this, what happens is that you will procrastinate whatever you are presently doing so that you do not have to get to the negative tasks that need to be done. Reverse the process and you will get through the day in much better fashion. The rationale for this is as follows: If you get your most unpleasant tasks done first, you will always be working toward the more pleasant tasks. Usually, the unpleasant tasks are the very tasks that will lead you toward your goal.

3. At the end of each day make a list of tasks that need to be done to accomplish your goals. What are the priorities? Start each day by tackling the most important tasks first. By doing the most important tasks first your stress levels will be kept under control. This method will lead to greater accomplishment. You need to be careful that you don't fill up your day with tasks that you don't mind but that in fact do not assist you in personal and professional growth. One last point. As long as you are doing the most important things first you will be functioning at your optimal level. Knowing this should make you feel good.

4. Learn to plan ahead. Anticipate. Think about what you want to do in the immediate future as well as sometime in the distant future. Planning is critical to good time management. Your ability to plan assists you in concentrating your effort on achieving whatever tasks need to be accomplished. For example, when you come to the office, if

Foot in the Door

you have a lot of letter dictation to take care of, you should allow a certain period of time when there will not be distractions so that you and your secretary can get this job completed. You may also want to consider the purchase of a dictaphone. Too many times, an executive will dictate letters to his secretary and be interrupted many times. This wastes time, interrupts the train of thought and the flow of information. It would be preferable to identify a period of time when the secretary and the executive can be alone to take care of this job. They will do it quicker and more effectively. Planning ahead is critical to your success.

5. Review each day. Analyze your accomplishments. Look for positive as well as any negative feedback that may have come to you. By reviewing each day, you can see where you are going. You can analyze whether or not you are on course and determine if you have to make any changes. It is important for you to let in all of the positive

things that have occurred to you each day so that you maintain a positive self-image. On the other hand, where a negative has come your way, it is imperative for you to identify something good from that negative and to move on it. By so doing, you will have a high energy drive level and you will be keeping yourself on course as far as your personal and professional goals are concerned.

6. Identify both short-term goals and long-range goals. It is important for you to have short-term goals identified so that you can accomplish them in a short period of time. On the other hand, your short-term goals should be leading you toward long-range goals. As we mentioned in earlier chapters, as one achieves goals one develops more self-confidence. It also produces pictures in one's mind that will create energy and drive. It is this very energy and drive that will assist you in achieving your long-range goals.

7. Double up on time. Try to find logical combinations for using your time productively. Example: If you take the bus or train to work, use this time to read some reports or dictate into a dictaphone. The key here is that you probably will be sitting down anyway; therefore, you might as well use your time productively to do something that needs to be done. Doubling up on time is an excellent way to have more time at the end of the day to do other things.

8. Make use of bits of time. Small units of time can be used constructively. For example, when you are waiting in your doctor's office for an appointment, plan your day for the following day. Or when you go to the repair shop to pick up your car and it is necessary to wait 15 minutes, you could outline a report that you will be preparing the

Foot in the Door

following day. In any event, take advantage of bits of time. Most people feel that if they only have 10 or 15 minutes during portions of their day, they might as well just dilly-dally. This is poor time management. Take these little pieces of time to do something constructive. Doing this will add to the time you have available to yourself each day.

9. Learn to delegate responsibilities effectively. A major problem people have is not feeling comfortable in delegating responsibility. This is true both in the home and on the job. It is important for you to realize that there are others who can carry out responsibilities effectively, allowing you more time to do other things. Hence, it is critical for you to be able to teach others in your organization or your home to carry out responsibilities that need to be taken care of. This will free you and allow them to grow in their own way. Too many executives feel that they are the only ones who can do things. High performance people are those who have taught others to do many of the things that they do so that they can be doing other things that are more important. Do not be fooled by the notion that if others can carry out some of your responsibilities in your home or organization, you are not worthwhile. To the contrary, you have trained them well and this is a good indicator that you are in control of things. The person who has to do everything is the individual who will have little time to do the more important things and it is also the individual who will burn out. A good example of delegation in the home would be having the children and husband responsible for taking the garbage out, setting the table for dinner and cleaning the table after dinner, making the beds, and keeping their rooms picked up. Family mem-

bers need to be reminded every now and then that they are part of the organizational structure of the home and, therefore, have certain responsibilities to carry out. Such delegation can really work in the home, but it is important to be fair and firm in delegating tasks. Go for it.

10. Get started now. Don't procrastinate. Procrastination is one of the worst time offenders that I can think of. A major reason for people procrastinating is that they don't want to do what needs to be done. I suggest to people that, when they have to do things they do not want to do and they find themselves procrastinating, they need to picture the goal they are moving toward and realize that by doing whatever it is, they will achieve or arrive at that goal much sooner. One way to assist you in this is to make a sign that simply says, "Do it now!" Become a "do it now" person and you won't have time to dwell on tasks that you do not like doing. You will just get them done and move on. As I said earlier, if you are doing the uncomfortable things first and have a list of other things that are positive, you will be eager to work through the

uncomfortable tasks in order to get to the more positive tasks. In any event, the key to preventing procrastination is to become a "Do it now" person. So, do it now!

Symptoms of Poor Time Management

Rushing: When you rush you usually make mistakes which definitely waste time.

Lack of Planning: Learn to plan your activities so you are not covering the same ground over and over again. You also need to have a plan for the goals you intend to accomplish. As we said earlier, this will give you direction.

Chronic Vacillation Between Unpleasant Alternatives: Collect as much information as you can on each alternative and then make a decision and get on with it.

Frequently Missed Deadlines: When you get into a pattern of behavior that results in missing deadlines, it usually produces distress which results in wasting time. A major cause of missing deadlines is poor planning, rushing, vacillation, and negative thinking. You can control these factors and become a person who meets deadlines.

Feeling Overwhelmed: You may be trying to do too much at one time, which can create fear, anxiety, and doubt. When this occurs you may be unable to work on the task at hand, which in turn may lead to burnout.

Fatigue: When you realize you are falling behind you probably will begin to worry, which will drain your energy and drive levels. The result will be physical and mental fatigue.

Examine these symptoms of poor time management carefully. If you have any of them, apply the time management strategies which have been presented in this chapter. They can make a real difference. You can do it. It's just a decision away.

Making Time

The following list of ideas can be very helpful in making time.

Learn to Say No: Let people know when you are overextended. Tell them you would be willing to help at a later time if this would be helpful. Most people will accept this. If they choose not to, that is their dilemma.

Banish Low-Priority Tasks: Analyze how you are allocating your time and stop spending time on low-priority tasks.

Stop Being a Perfectionist: Just get the job done well. Get the point. Then you can move on to the next task.

Eliminate or Reduce Television Time: Check and see how much time you are spending watching or glaring at the television. If it is helping you to reach your goals by relaxing you or generating new ideas that you can use, fine. If, however, it doesn't assist you I would suggest you reduce the time you spend watching television.

Foot in the Door

Get Up Earlier: You may be surprised that you prefer getting up earlier. You will need to do this for two consecutive weeks to allow your body to adjust. The important point is for you to determine the correct amount of sleep that you require to be most effective. If this can be reduced, Great. If not, that's O.K. too.

Review each of these ideas and apply those that will help you gain some time. **Write these ideas down now.**

Things I Can Do To Gain Time

_____
_____
_____
_____
_____
_____
_____
_____

The information presented in this chapter was designed to assist you in taking control of your time. Once you have control of your time, you will be well on your way to achieving the goals you have set for yourself. Good Luck! Do it now.

__Write down the Key Ideas you have learned about how you are currently using your time and how you should be using your time. For each idea write down a positive action you can take to put yourself into a positive growth pattern.__

Chapter XII

Ten Principles of Self-Power

During the past five years I have conducted many **Self-Power Concepts** seminars where I have used a variety of principles to assist people in their personal and professional growth. During this time, I have crystallized ten **Self-Power** principles which I have found to be extremely effective in my own life, and from data obtained from participants during the past five years it is clear to me that these principles work when applied by any individual. I would therefore like to suggest that you read each principle carefully, examine each illustration, and then apply the principles in your own life. I can assure you that within four to six weeks you will see major changes in the way you are behaving. Most importantly, you will be moving in a positive direction and you will be happy with yourself. I have had many participants who have graduated from **Self-Power Concepts** seminars write to me and call me to state that, as they became self-powered, people around them gravitated toward them and liked being with them. Many of these people were people within their own families, which made this change all the more important and beautiful. Here, then, are the ten principles of **Self-Power** living.

The following format will be utilized in presenting each principle:

> First, I will state the principle;
> Second, I will give you a summary statement which describes and defines the principle;
> Third, I will discuss and illustrate the principle.

PRINCIPLE 1: Principle of Return

Summary Statement: Give and you will receive.

Illustration: It is clear to me that people need to be willing to give of themselves and give things that they possess to others. When you are willing to do this, you will receive far more than what you have given. It is important to note that when you give, it will come back to you in many ways. You may receive from the person to whom you have given; however, in many cases you will receive from others you do not even know. In any event, you can be assured you will receive when you follow this principle.

In one program that I conducted, I had a participant come back to me after two weeks and state that she had been giving to her roommate during the past two weeks, but her roommate had not given her anything in return. This is not the way to apply the principle. When you give, the mere fact that you have given is the reward. In return, you will receive from others, but when this

Foot in the Door

will occur will vary. Your attitude toward giving should be that you enjoy giving and not that you give to get. In reality you will get a much larger return than what you have given, but it is imperative that your mind-set be that you give because you choose to give. That's it.

Let me reiterate. You will receive far more than what you have given.

PRINCIPLE 2: Principle of Acquisition

YOU MAY WANT TO "DELETE" THEM

Summary Statement: Get rid of what you don't want to make room for what you do want.

Illustration: Go through your closet and count the number of shirts or blouses you have that you haven't worn for the past year. Why not get get rid of them? Give them to your local church. Get a tax receipt. And now, make room for some new clothing. You may say, "That's silly!" Let me assure you that what I am saying is not silly. Do what I say and you will be amazed at how many new pieces of clothing you will acquire that you really desire. What purpose or use are those pieces of clothing serving you if you never wear them? Make some room for new pieces of clothing.

Utilize the same principle in other areas. If you "fly off the handle," why not replace that with being calm and cool? If you would like to speak in front of large groups without getting nervous, why not get some training in that area? Get rid of the self-image that you can't speak in front of large groups and replace it with the self-image that you can. Believe me, you will be able to. Now, don't carry this principle to an extreme. For instance, if you have a three-year-old car don't sell it and expect the next day to have a new car in your driveway. That is not what I am saying and I'm certain you understand that. To recapitulate, when you get rid of material things and personal behaviors that you do **not** want and put some time and effort into what you **do** want, you will be amazed at how rapidly you will acquire those material things and personal characteristics you desire. It is an exciting venture. Try it; you'll like it!

PRINCIPLE 3: Principle of Propulsion

Summary Statement: Decide what you want; define it clearly and specifically.

Write it down!

Illustration: Have you ever found yourself going from one task to another and never seeming to make headway in any of them? This typically results because you have not decided on a specific

Foot in the Door

destination or point at which you want to arrive. The principle of propulsion states that, once you identify a point at which you want to arrive, your energies can be put forth in a way that will get you to that point. Hence, it is imperative for people to decide what they want and, in doing this, they should define it clearly and specifically. By writing it down, it is clear as to what they really want. Once this is accomplished, they will have the energy and drive to move in that direction because they know where they want to go. Many people, however, are afraid to do this because they fear failure. Little do they know that if they wrote down their goal and concentrated on it by visualizing pictures, they would create enough energy and drive which exists within them to achieve the goal and, therefore, in fact, not be a failure.

PRINCIPLE 4: Principle of Power Pictures

Summary Statement: Get a clear mental picture of exactly what you want; infuse it with emotion; and hold on!

Illustration: The key to power pictures is simple. Once you lock in your mind what it is you want, these pictures will produce emotions and the emotions will result in effective action to move the human system in a direction that will achieve the desired picture.

Illustration: If you desire a certain type of automobile and begin to picture yourself in the automobile via the affirmation process, you will automatically begin to do things to get that automobile. The truth is that if you look at your personality and the way you behave, many of the things you do are based on the way you see yourself. These are power pictures. What most people do not realize is that you can create the power pictures of things you desire whether they be materialistic or personal characteristics. Continue to focus on such power pictures and the human system will begin to move in that direction.

A few more illustrations may be helpful. A failure sees himself as a failure. A person with low self-confidence sees himself as a person with low self-confidence. On the reciprocal end of things, an individual who is an effective administrator sees himself as an effective administrator. A mother who considers herself to be a competent mother taking care of her children, her home, and her husband sees herself this way. Those mothers, on the other hand, who are having stress and depression as a result of being a mother see themselves this way. It all happens in the mind, and power pictures can be the key to unleashing boundless energy and drive which, in effect, move the individual to doing the things that need to be done to arrive at the pictures they wrote in their minds.

PRINCIPLE 5: Principle of Ordainment

Summary Statement: What you verbalize will happen.

Illustration: Have you ever noticed people saying things like, "I am clumsy." "I always have accidents in the winter." "I don't have any self-confidence." "I always get a cold around Christmas-time." "I know I will get nervous when the boss calls on me to speak in front of the group"? What is common in all of these illustrations is simple. The individual is using words or stating words which trigger pictures in the mind which result in the action or behavior that the words are stating. Hence, individuals need to learn not to say things they do not want to happen to them or to say things concerning characteristics they do not desire such as, "I don't have any self-confidence." As long as the

Foot in the Door

individuals persist in this type of speech, they will continue to lack self-confidence.

On the other hand, if people are willing to begin to speak positively about the characteristics they would like to possess, such words trigger pictures which are positive and the mind will then move the human system into action so that these pictures become a reality. It is therefore important for you to use words that are positive so that they will move you in a direction you want to go.

PRINCIPLE 6: Principle of Performance

Summary Statement: Do it now!

Illustration: Too many individuals find that they hesitate to take the first step. The reason for this is that they are afraid. I have found that when you follow the principle of performance and learn that when something can be done you do it NOW, the individual is able to dissipate a great deal of stress. People also have the capacity to get much more accomplished simply because they are not thinking and worrying about what they ought to be doing but instead are doing the very thing that needs to be done. This allows them to be able to accomplish important tasks and get them on to the next one. What they are doing is getting into action and not worrying about inaction.

One way to become a "do it now" person is simply to make a little sign that you can see every day. Put it on your desk, the dashboard of your car, or on your refrigerator, but someplace where it will be a constant reminder to you to DO IT NOW! You will be amazed at how much more you will accomplish by following this principle.

PRINCIPLE 7: Principle of Wholeheartedness

Summary Statement: Give everything you've got to everything you do.

Illustration: Learn how to get totally involved. Don't be a person who sits around and says, "Well, I'll give my all to this, but only part of me to that." If it's worth doing, it's worth doing wholeheartedly. This will generate enthusiasm and excitement, motivation and, most important, energy and drive. Even those tasks you dislike doing, do them with wholeheartedness. Get in there and get it done. Do it rapidly and get on to the next thing. Too many people are involved in tasks they give only partial effort to. This drains the human system and doesn't allow it to get on with those things it would prefer doing. Remember, you will always have certain tasks that need to be done which you dislike doing. Do them anyway because they need to be done; then get on with those tasks that will move you in the direction you want to go.

PRINCIPLE 8: Principle of Faith

Summary Statement: Faith is believing in something without evidence.

Illustration: As we move through life, many things will happen to us that we really cannot explain. Goal-setting, to a certain degree, is faith. It's believing before the goal is attained that you have the ability and skills to attain that goal. What makes an individual believe this? In my opinion, it is faith. It is believing that something can come or occur even though the specific facts are not evident.

As one reads literature, the arts, the sciences and history, it is all too clear that faith is a powerful force in the events that have occured in these areas. Faith is powerful. It is powerful because it allows the human system to move in directions that many people would be unwilling to move toward if they had to have all the evidence available before taking the first step.

I have found in my own life and in the lives of many people that it is necessary to identify what you want to become and to have faith in yourself. Once you have done this you will muster the energy and drive to move in ways that will allow you to reach your goals. You must believe it before it occurs. You must feel it before it occurs. You must be willing to believe before there is evidence. This is faith, a powerful force. Use it and it will allow you to become the person you really want to be.

PRINCIPLE 9: Principle of Self-Discipline

Summary Statement: Do what needs to be done when it ought to be done whether you like it or not.

Illustration: Many times I have found myself in a situation where I did not want to do something that needed to be done. I was always able to find reasons why I ought to be doing something else. This caused me to procrastinate in those things that should have been done in order to move me in the direction I wanted to go. When I learned the principle of self-discipline, many interesting things occurred. The most important thing I learned was that when I learned to do what needs to be done when it ought to be done, I was able to get a lot more accomplished and my stress levels went way down and the tasks really didn't seem that difficult. I also had to learn that I had total control over my self-discipline. When I controlled this part of my mental thinking, I became more effective and was happier. When I did not follow this principle, I found myself off-course, less happy and under great distress. I also found that many of the things I thought I would not like doing, I actually enjoyed doing. Follow this principle and you will be amazed at the transition and transformation of your behavior in a positive direction.

PRINCIPLE 10: Principle of Tenacity

Summary Statement: I will until...

Illustration: How close were you to success the last time you decided to quit? Do you know? Not really; you never know when you quit. Hence, the principle of tenacity is critical to success in any area of endeavor. When you decide to follow this principle, there is nothing that you will not complete. You will learn that, once you set your mind to completing a task, it can be done if you have decided to do it.

People who choose not to follow the principle of tenacity will become individuals who frequently do not complete tasks. This occurs because this becomes their reality structure. Hence, it is normal, okay, just like them, not to complete tasks. This becomes the foundation of their reality structure and they are the individuals who are the low performers. You can be a **Self-Powered Person** when you choose to be.

The preceding principles are powerful. They can change your life in a positive direction. Examine them. Reread their meaning. Look at each illustration and ask yourself what impact these principles would have on you, your behavior, and your future if you chose to follow them. I assure you that the impact will be great. The results will be positive. You and the people around you will be glad you chose to follow them. ***Go for it.***

Putting It All Together

We have come a long way together. I have shared the key concepts that make an individual a **Self-Powered Person**. You have read these concepts and have completed many assessment activities to give you a clear picture of where you are now and, more importantly, where you want to be. The ten principles of **Self-Power Living** succinctly comprise the main ideas in this book. I am confident that when you apply the concepts in this book they will change your life dramatically in a positive direction. **YOU HAVE YOUR FOOT IN THE DOOR.** You have already taken the first step by reading this book. The next step is to apply the concepts to your personal and professional life. When you decide to take action you will begin to attain big benefits.

Finally, I would like to share with you the best criteria that will indicate that you are in a positive growth pattern and that you are becoming a **Self-Powered Person**. People around you will tell you that there is something different about you. They are right. You are different, you are in control and **Self-Powered**. Your new thinking pattern and actions will be noticed by your family, friends and acquaintances. They may ask you what you are on. Tell them **SPC (Self-Power Concepts)**. That's when you will really know that you are applying the concepts of **Self-Power**. The road you will travel as a **Self-Powered Person** is Exciting, Rewarding, and Growth Producing.

Enjoy The Journey

BIBLIOGRAPHY

Allen, James, *As a Man Thinketh*. New York: Grosset & Dunlap, Inc., 1959; Lakemont, Ga.: CSA Press, new edition, 1975, softcover.

Berne, Eric. *Beyond Games and Script: Selections from His Major Writings*. Edited by Claude Steiner and Carmen Kerr. New York: Grove Press, Inc., 1976; Grove Press, Inc., 1977, paperback.

_____. *Games People Play: The Psychology of Human Relationships*. New York: Grove Press, Inc., 1964; Grove Press, Inc., 1964, paperback; Random House, Inc., Ballantine Books, Inc., 1976, paperback.

Briggs, Dorothy Corkille. *Your Child's Self-Esteem: The Key to His Life*. New York: Doubleday & Co., Inc., 1970; Doubleday & Co., Inc., Dolphin Books, 1975, paperback.

Bristol, Claude. *The Magic of Believing*. Englewood Cliffs, N.J.: Prentice-Hall, Inc., 1957; New York: Cornerstone Library, Inc., 1967, paperback.

Carnegie, Dale. *How to Win Friends and Influence People*. New York: Simon & Schuster, Inc., 1936; Pocket Books, Inc., 1977, paperback.

Cooper, Kenneth H. *The Aerobics Way*. New York: Bantam Books, Inc., 1978.

Frankl, Viktor E. *Man's Search for Meaning*. Revised edition. Boston, Mass.: Beacon Press, Inc., 1963; New York: Pocket Books, Inc., 1975, paperback.

Fromm, Erich. *The Art of Loving.* New York: Harper & Row Publishers, Inc., Perennial Library, 1974, paperback.

Gardiner, John W. *Excellence: Can We Be Equal and Excellent Too.* New York: Harper & Row Publishers, Inc., 1961; Harper & Row Publishers, Inc., Perennial Library, 1971, paperback.

———. *Self-Renewal: The Individual and the Innovative Society.* New York: Harper & Row Publishers, Inc., 1964; Harper & Row Publishers, Inc., Colophon Books, 1964, paperback; Harper & Row, Publishers, Inc., Perennial Library, 1971, paperback.

Gibran, Kahlil. *The Prophet.* New York: Alfred A. Knopf, Inc., 1923.

Glasser, William, M.D. *Schools Without Failure.* New York: Harper & Row Publishers, Inc., 1969; Harper & Row Publishers, Inc., Perennial Library, 1975, paperback.

Harris, Thomas A., M.D. *I'm OK — You're OK: A Practical Guide to Transactional Analysis.* New York: Harper & Row Publishers, Inc., 1969; Avon Books, 1973, paperback.

Hill, Napoleon. *Think and Grow Rich.* New York: Hawthorne Books, Inc., 1966; Fawcett World Library, 1976, paperback.

Hoffer, Eric. *The True Believer.* New York: Harper & Row Publishers, Inc., 1951; Harper & Row Publishers, Inc., Perennial Library, 1966, paperback.

James, Muriel, and Jongeward, Dorothy. *Born to Win: Transactional Analysis with Gestalt Experiments.* Reading, Mass.: Addison-Wesley Publishing Co., Inc., 1971.

Lao Tzu. *Tao Te Ching.* Translated by D. C. Lau. New York: Penguin Books, Inc., 1964, paperback.

Lederer, William J., and Jackson, Don D. *The Mirages of Marriage.* New York: W.W. Norton & Company, Inc., 1968.

Lindbergh, Anne Morrow. *Gift from the Sea.* New York: Pantheon Books, 1955; Random House, Inc., Vintage Trade Books, 1965, paperback.

Maltz, Maxwell, M.D. Psycho-Cybernetics: The New Way to a Successful Life. Englewood Cliffs, N.J.: Prentice-Hall, Inc., 1960; Pocket Books, Inc., paperback.

Maslow, Abraham H. *The Farther Reaches of Human Nature.* New York: Viking Press, Inc., 1971.

Nightingale, Earl. *This Is Earl Nightingale.* New York: Doubleday & Co., Inc., 1969.

Naisbitt, John. *Megatrends.* New York: Warner Books, Inc. 1982.

Osborn, Alex F. *Applied Imagination: Priciples and Procedures of Creative Problem-Solving.* 3rd edition. New York: Charles Scribner's Sons, 1963, paperback.

Peters, Thomas J., Waterman, Robert H. *In Search of Excellence.* New York: Warner Books, Inc., 1982.

Selye, Hans. *Stress Without Distress.* Philadelphia: J. B. Lippincott Co., 1974; New York: New American Library, Signet Books, 1975, paperback.

ABOUT THE AUTHOR

Ph. D. in Health Science from the University of New Mexico

Consultant and trainer for more than one hundred organizations

Former President of New York State Public Health Association, Northeastern Regional Affiliate

Received "Outstanding Young Alumni Award," Pittsburg State University

Developed and implemented a specialized **Self-Power Concepts** program for Viet Nam Veterans and their wives

Has authored a number of articles for professional journals and written material for several health education textbooks

Is a frequent speaker for schools, community health agencies, hospitals, sales organizations, Cub Scouts, and religious groups

Is married with two young sons, Tony and Joey

Enjoys fishing, swimming, golf, and rowing

Guest Speaker

Organizations interested in having Dr. Pelizza speak to their groups or provide in-house training and seminars on motivation, self-concept development for improving performance, and stress management should write to:

Self-Power Concepts
Box 225
North Chatham, New York 12132

Attention: Schools and Corporations

Books are available at quantity discounts with bulk purchase for educational, business, or sales promotion use. You may order single copies prepaid direct from **Self-Power Concepts** for $12.00.

Another Book by Dr. Pelizza

THOUGHTS

to make you THINK
...and FEEL BETTER

By John J. Pelizza, Ph.D.

...Is a book of positive quotes for daily living to help you do better and feel better.

ORDER FORM

Qty	Item	Unit Price	Total Price
	FOOT in the DOOR	12.00	
	THOUGHTS to make you THINK and FEEL BETTER	12.00	

MAIL ORDER FORM AND CHECK PAYABLE TO:
SELF-POWER CONCEPTS
BOX 225
NORTH CHATHAM, NEW YORK 12132

NAME _____

ADDRESS _____

CITY _____ STATE _____

Discounts available for quantities over 25.
Write for quote.   ZIP _____